"Women will control 2/3rds of the nation's wealth within 5 years. This is the quintessential roadmap to capturing this untapped market of $14 trillion in assets."

Kimberly Medaglia
One Smooth Stone

"There is so much money in motion now and most advisors are working the same overcrowded, overfished pond. Women are a large open pool of clients. This is a great fishing tool. Go for it!"

Michelle Alberda
Author: *SkirtWorking: How to Network Using SKIRT*

"For you to be part of a women's financial life, you need to understand the unfortunate barriers they face in the workforce, realize how they must learn to communicate with male colleagues and balance their personal lives with their careers. This book opens the door to understand how best to work with the largest work force in America."

Rich DeSalvo
Author: *The Power of Pain*

"Women are among the most powerful decision makers in the industry. Barbara and Tony illustrate ways to build your practice and realize the financial potential within this influential group."

Alethia Bapis Chatzis
The Bapis Group/HighTower Advisors

"We all have to up our game in educating and working cooperatively with clients. This is not just an issue for women. The skills that are needed for women clients are now needed for all clients. The old equations don't fit now. The numbers game is obsolete. The old style marketing and sales tactics never worked for women and now they don't work for men either."

Beth Rosenwald
Senior Vice President and Branch Director
RBC Wealth Management

THE
$14 TRILLION
WOMAN

Your Essential Guide to Engaging the Female Client

By

Barbara A. Kay MA, LPC, RCC

&

Anthony J. DiLeonardi, RCC

ISBN: 1-4392-3064-1
ISBN-13: 9781439230640
Library of Congress Control Number: 2009901802

Visit www.booksurge.com to order additional copies.

Table of Contents

Foreword

I grew up in a family of boys and we resided in a neighborhood of boys. Instead of four seasons, our lives revolved around three: baseball season, football season and basketball season.

Today, more than thirty years later, I'm surrounded by females. I live in an old Victorian home in Greenwich, Connecticut with my wife, our two daughters and our dog, who is--you guessed it--female. My daughters are both cheerleaders and sometimes we have 25 or more teenage girls in our home.

Given my present surroundings, I've had ample opportunities to observe female behavior. Here's what I've noticed.

Movies. The joke in our home is that Dad only likes movies with helicopters; such as, *Behind Enemy Lines*, *Blackhawk Down*, or anything with Bruce Willis. The women around me like movies with Hugh Grant. These movies put me to sleep in nanoseconds.

Remote controls. The women in my life could care less who's holding the remote (except for when I mistakenly hit the channel button instead of the volume). I, on the other hand, feel anxious without it.

Talking. The women around me use a lot more words than the men I know. When men tell the story of how they met their wives, it takes about four minutes, tops. When the women tell the story, it takes at least 20 minutes and it's generally a lot more interesting.

Any reasonable observer can see that men and women are different. The Bible says God made Eve from Adam's rib. I think it must've been a female who said that God knew he could do better on the second try.

From neuroscience we know that men and women have different levels of hormones in their bodies. Testosterone and estrogen are the hormones we hear most about. But they are just the beginning. There is also dopamine, serotonin, oxytocin, epinephrine and norepinephrine, to name just a few. Differing levels of these hormones make men and women feel and behave differently, just as the varying the amounts of the same ingredients in two cakes can make them considerably different.

Given the differences between men and women, if you're a male and you're selling to and helping female clients, it would be irrational not to be *intentional* about how to understand these differences and successfully address them. To ignore this is to commit self-sabotage. And that's exactly what many financial advisors do.

Thankfully, Tony DiLeonardi and Barbara Kay have made it easy for you to understand how best to sell and provide financial advice to women. Tony brings decades of experience on Wall Street and Barbara brings insights from psychology. They are the dream team for a book on this topic. You will be better for reading it.

Michael Lee Stallard
President and Co-founder, E Pluribus Partners
Primary Author, *Fired Up or Burned Out: How to Reignite Your Team's Passion, Creativity and Productivity*

Preface

From Barbara

It was years before I actually read introductory sections to books. I was too eager to dive into the core of the book to spend time on anything but the actual chapters. Now, I find these sections can add greatly to the experience of the book. So, if you would like to add to your experience – read away. If you want to dive right in, go ahead and skip this portion. We know what it is like to be in a hurry for the meat of the topic.

The journey to writing this book developed over time with multiple twists and turns. Like any good journey there were ups and downs, highs and lows before we reached our destination. The important part of the journey is why I started and the treasure that was found at the end – this book.

This book frankly begged to be written. For more than a year, I kept bumping into the topic in all facets: the question, the need, the customer desire, the misperceptions, the services gap, the opportunities waiting and the solutions. Your peers, in particular, kept bringing me this topic. Of course, my natural curiosity took over and I began to send out some feelers: Is there a need for this? The response was dramatic and emphatic – YES!

The project was in the formation stages when Tony and I joined forces. I have been thrilled and delighted to partner with Tony on this project. I am no expert in financial services. Tony has years of expertise in the financial services field and gives the added benefit of the male viewpoint. My professional expertise is in relationships, communication and psychology. I understand women, building relationships and the great service financial advisors bring to women. Together we make an excellent team!

Barbara A. Kay, MA, LPC, RCC

From Tony

Like Barbara, this book was and still is a journey for me. I kept seeing opportunities in the marketplace and in my own life to do things a bit differently. I grew up in a home full of guys. My parents had six boys and only one girl — it was a guy's house! What do I have to offer to the female consumer? Not much. I continue to learn where, why and how we differ from our counterparts. Today, with my wife, we have three daughters (and one son). Turnabout is fair play, as my son and I attempt to understand the ladies in our house. I'm on this journey of life to understand, to stretch and to make a difference. For you, the excellent investment professional, the journey is the same. This journey usually leads to improving and achieving higher levels of productivity. Be open to the possibility that there are new things to learn. This book is a sincere effort to offer advisors the opportunity to genuinely and respectfully serve the female marketplace.

Anthony J. DiLeonardi, RCC

Acknowledgements

From Barbara

My thanks to Tony for partnering with me, to Claymore Securities for supporting us in this project and to my life-long friend Tim Ursiny, the founder of Advantage Coaching & Training. This was a team effort! Lastly, my deepest gratitude to Bob, my extraordinary husband, who supports me in all things!

From Tony

Thanks to Barbara Kay for including me in her idea and work. Thanks to Dave Hooten for all the opportunities. Most importantly, thanks to my wife, Diane, who puts up with me and who never laughed out loud when I told her I was writing a book on females.

From Barbara and Tony

We benefited from many generous supporters during the development of this book. We are tremendously grateful for our **Live on Street** contributors: Michelle Alberda, Patricia Bates, Ernest Dorsey, David Hellinger, Craig Holmes, Jodi Manthei and Beth Rosenwald. These folks graciously offered their time and experience for all our benefit. It was thrilling to see our written words come alive through the applied innovation of these folks. We hope their experiences are equally powerful for you. We also want to thank those who kindly offered advice and encouragement: Alethia Bapis Chatzis, Rick Capozzi, Rich DeSalvo, Amy Florian, Kimberly Medaglia and Keith VanderVeen. We offer special thanks to the author of our forward Michael Lee Stallard for his noble spirit and personal touch. The generosity of all these exceptional people is profoundly appreciated. Last but not least, we offer sincere thanks to those who diligently helped refine our words and presentation: Todd Donat, Sue Gage, Kristan Mulley, Hollie Murrin, Carole Smith and Marla Ursiny. Thank you to all our supporters. We are tremendously grateful!

Evolutionary Bio

Neuropsychology

Introduction

A Reader's Guide

Who Are We Addressing?

In writing this book we had to decide, who is our audience? Are we talking to men or women or both? This book has value for male and female professionals and we could have used space writing alternately to both viewpoints. Instead, we decided to be more direct. We assumed that if the reader is seeking information on female clients, then the reader is probably not a female. Women advisors already have inside knowledge about women. Therefore, our viewpoint addresses male readers.

For those readers who are women, we hope this book serves to confirm your inside knowledge. We also hope that it gives you added confidence to go against the grain of male-focused practices you encounter in your industry. If we confirm your intuition about women and give you more freedom to succeed, tremendous! Use this book to become even more successful! Thanks in advance for your understanding that we're speaking to the guys in how we present the material.

OK, for you male readers, we are speaking to you! We will show you how to be successful in attracting, retaining and serving female clients.

A Word of Caution

Any time there is a discussion of general trends within a specific group the threat status instantly elevates to red alert. We immediately start looking for language land mines and everyone becomes hyper-sensitive. People naturally begin to hedge their words with multiple qualifiers in order to prevent offense. Sometimes this so greatly dilutes the message that it's nearly unintelligible, rendering it mostly worthless. We decided to take a different approach. We directly refer to overall gender trends as we discuss male and female clients. We do this for the sake of clarity fully recognizing the limits of such simplicity. Broad generalizations have some usefulness in helping people separate out big ideas, but their utility is limited. They only help with rough estimations, beyond that we must pay attention to the individual more than the pattern. We firmly believe there are vast individual differences within and across genders. Please remember, not every man and woman fits the general tendencies. We also employ literary license with our phrasing. We really did not want this to read like a text book, precise, detached and boring! Please allow our lighthearted tone without misunderstanding our intent. We have the highest respect for both men and women. We are committed to helping others succeed in business and have the greatest regard for all the clients we serve and all you serve. Our goal is to help you expand your skills and succeed in a way that is enjoyable and practical.

How the Book Is Organized

This book is organized for people who want to get to the bottom line! We try to quickly answer the top three questions of all readers:

1. What is this chapter about?

2. What is the bottom line?

3. What do I do?

It's also detailed enough that you can delve deeper and gain fuller mastery of the subject. This is an increasingly fast-paced world where most communication is condensed into bullet points. We don't want to lose our readers in too much detail. At the same time, we want you to develop the highest skill-level possible. Developing successful female client relationships takes attention to detail and practice.

With that balance in mind, we begin by highlighting the huge opportunity awaiting you. We want to connect with your core motivations:

✓ What's in it for me?

✓ Why do I care?

After making a convincing case for the reward being worth your effort, the remaining chapters provide a guide to attract and retain the female client. Then, we round out the topic with the details on how to expand your female client base. Each chapter is organized with features to help you find quick answers, practical solutions, background data and illuminating anecdotes. You will find the following sections in each chapter:

Rapid Rundown. A quick chapter overview

Nuts and Bolts. The main chapter topic with data, stories, examples and skills

She Said/He Said. Barbara and Tony's perspectives

Live on the Street. Interviews with your peers

The Bottom Line. A summary of main points

Individual Application. Opportunity to note personal application

Call to Action. What you can do. Now!

Personal Goals & Action Steps. A worksheet for personal planning

About the Facts and Our Opinions

All of the data in the book was researched from reliable sources. We did not conduct original research for this project. Instead, we relied on the high-quality work of others. You'll find facts listed in bullet points and referenced in the text. It's clear when we're using other sources. However, in the interest of simplicity and readability, we did not footnote every data point. At the same time, it is important readers have confidence in the material and we honor our sources. At the end of the book you will find a list of all our sources. We also clearly indicate where we assert an opinion. We make it easy for you to differentiate between researched data and our professional viewpoint. Opinions are preceded by phrases like, "We believe...". Our opinion's are solely our own. We do not presume to represent any other person or organization. Ultimately, our goal is it to give you the facts, skills, tools and confidence to successfully build a practice filled with clients who want and need your services.

CHAPTER 1

Is She Worth It?

Rapid Rundown

If increasing the number of female clients is a new initiative, you need ample incentive to change direction. Why should you step outside your comfort zone? This chapter outlines the considerable consumer clout of women and the vast opportunity that awaits you.

Nuts and Bolts

Why Should I Bother?

Let me (Tony) share a true and perfect story for why, I believe, we have great opportunity when we reach out to female clients.

My wife manages all our daily finances. *(There, I admitted it—but guys, I promise I am not unique.)* She is bright, organized and gifted to this role. Even though I have spent much of my career in financial services, Diane controls the checkbook, while we share in the long-term investment decisions. Unfortunately, most people assume the opposite. Some would be highly embarrassed if they knew the error of their assumptions. For example, our family makes regular contributions to a particular missionary organization. Each year, my wife Diane, writes, signs and mails the check. Yet, I get a personal thank-you card annually addressed to me and written to me alone. We are grateful that a key leader takes the time to write a personal thank you. Unfortunately, every year it's obvious that he believes I have written the check. At first it was humorous, but over the years it's become annoying. We would like to correct the mistake, but don't want this leader to feel embarrassed.

Unfortunately, these missteps are too common. The female advisors we spoke to are frequently approached by women clients who've had bad experiences with male advisors. Unfortunately, there is nothing in financial services training that teaches advisors how to deal with the human side of the business. This lack of relationship training has a negative impact on the bottom line. I (Barbara) recently spoke with Amy Florian, the founder of her own consulting firm, Corgenius. Amy is a thanatologist. A thanatologist is an expert in grieving. Amy works in financial services, teaching advisors how to help grieving clients. She shared with me a startlingly statistic on the importance of building relationships. Research shows that 70% of widows switch advisors after their husbands die. Surprised by this statistic, I decided to check this out in my own social circle. I asked married friends, would they stay with their advisor should their husband leave or die? The response was disturbing. Many had absolutely no relationship with the advisor and had no reason to stay. My social circle reinforced the data. Too many women are not connected to their advisors. Something is seriously amiss if women are leaving male advisors in droves because of no connection or worse fleeing bad experiences.

Some of you may be wondering if any of this matters. Why would you bother with women clients anyway? Good question! Why should you? Some readers have been highly successful focusing on traditional methods. After all this worked for a good long time. It may seem like too much effort to change course now. For those, we have a question. Considering recent events in the financial industry (2008-2009), how many can rely on things that used to work? Even more, how many can afford to dismiss more than half the client population? If your practice has grown in the last year, if it is humming with profit and productivity and you can go along without innovation, go ahead and shut the book. The innovators can win a chunk of the $14 **trillion** (*yes, trillion!*) in assets American women control.

What's a Trillion?

$ If you spent one million dollars per day, it would take 2,740 years to spend a trillion dollars.

$ If you tried to count to one trillion (one number per second), it would take you 32,000 years to reach one trillion.

$ Traveling at the speed of light, it would take two months to cover a trillion miles.

$ One trillion dollars, stacked in one dollar bills, would make a stack 67,866 miles high--more than one-quarter of the way to the moon.

Startling Facts: The Impact of the Female Dollar

Women have serious consumer clout! Consider this:

✓ American women are the largest consumer group in the world. The next biggest group is the entire country of Japan.

✓ Women account for 64% of the U.S. gross domestic product.

✓ Women are responsible for 85% of **all** purchases.

That's a lot of money running through the fingers of women! Women are a huge customer base. However, before we get too far into the data, we want you to take an honest look at your client base. In order to get an unbiased evaluation of your practice, it's important that we take a snapshot before you're influenced by much new information. We also think it will be more powerful for you to do it now and set it aside for the moment. Later you can go back with fresh eyes and evaluate what it means for you. Let's take a brief moment to assess how you are doing with women clients.

Female Market Test

Using the blank pie chart below, indicate the demographics of your current practice. Draw a line to indicate the percentage of married couples within your practice. Mark that segment with an "M". Now mark off another segment for single males with "SM". Finally complete the chart with "SW" representing the percentage of single women. You may have some remaining clients representing businesses or other entities, which can be indicated with an "O" for other.

Client Demographics

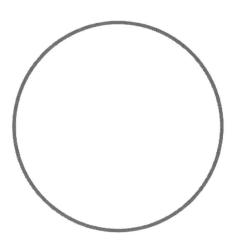

Female Market Reality

If you are doing well, the percentage of female clients in your practice (both married and single) will generally reflect the demographic found in the population at large.

According to U.S. Census Bureau, fifty-two percent of adult women are single. If your practice were to reflect American demographics, it would look something like this:

United States Population Demographics

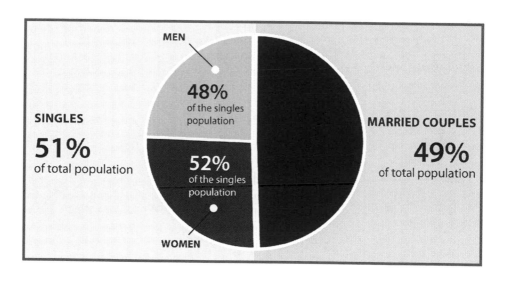

A Waiting Market

Nobody expects a financial services practice to perfectly reflect the American demographic. However, it is a measure of how well you're doing in attracting female investors. If you've successfully attracted and retained women clients, your practice will come close to the following demographics for individual clients:

➢ More than 25% will be single women.

➢ Half will be married women.

➢ The smallest group will be single men.

In addition, you will have a strong client relationship with the married women (equally as strong as your relationship with their husbands). If this is not the case, then there is great room for developing more and better female client connections. In fact, there are **6 million more** women than men in this country. In total, there are **115 million adult women** needing financial services. That is a deep vein of available female client business.

Treasure Hidden in Plain Sight

If you were not aware of these gigantic numbers, don't feel bad. There's been a seismic shift in the social and economic structure over the last several decades. In addition, so much media attention has focused on the lag in women's earning power (women's salaries are still only 77% of men's) less attention has been paid to the rise of female economic power. Even more, there are cultural myths about women and money that are hard to shake.

Myth: Women Are Irrational and Frivolous with Money

The cultural myths about women and money are easy to uncover. Do a simple search on Amazon the website for books about "women and money". We found a long list of advice books. Examples include: *Women & Money: Owning the Power to Control Your Destiny* by Suze Orman (2007) , *Money, A Memoir: Women, Emotions, and Cash* by Liz Perle (2006) or *Prince Charming Isn't Coming: How Women Get Smart About Money* by Barbara Stanny (2007). Many how-to books are published to help women become skilled at money management.

Next, we searched "men and money". Guess what? We found zero how-to books for men about handling money. The list was peppered with historical accounts and fiction titles but no financial advice books for men. The only advice books that appeared in our search for "men and money" were books directed at women about men: *Girlfriends Talk About Men: Sex, Money, Power* by Carmen Renee Berry and Tamara Traeder (2003) as an example. What impression do these titles portray? Would you assume that women are generally intelligent, objective, effective, strategic and successful at managing money? Absolutely not! These titles reflect the common myth that women can't manage money!

The impression is that women are too emotional, frivolous and irrational to effectively handle money. Anita Hamilton *(Time-Australia,* 4/16/2007) succinctly describes the effect of these myth-based advice books:

> "All these books claim to help empower women, but they wind up doing exactly the opposite. Most egregiously, they exaggerate women's financial foibles at a time when we are making more money than ever before."

These books perpetuate the myth by focusing on emotional issues, implying that women are primarily emotionally driven. They give the strong impression that women are too irrational to be good investors.

Reality vs. Myth

In our professional experience men and women are equally influenced by their emotions. Does anyone agree? Our Amazon search did disclose one popular book that displays confidence in women's money aptitude. In *Smart Women Finish Rich: 9 Steps to Achieving Financial Security and Funding Your Dreams* (2002), it is clear that David Bach firmly believes women make better investors than men. In his experience, women are **more** thoughtful and **less** emotionally driven than men. In fact, studies do support the notion of gender differences in investing behavior. Women appear to invest differently than men. Women tend to be more risk averse and invest more conservatively. Also, men and women tend to perceive their investments differently. Men are more likely to be over confident in their financial abilities and overestimate their success. In contrast, women display less confidence in investment decision-making and underestimate their success. None of the studies indicate that women are careless or irrational when making investment decisions. If anything, they are more thoughtful, not less.

She Said/He Said:
Are Women More Emotional About Money?

Barbara:
As a professional, trained in psychology, I understand the power of emotions. Emotions directly impact success in investing and in life. Too many consultants and programs focus on teaching practice management skills. People think more information is the key, but more information is frequently not the solution. I compare it to the challenge of eating well and exercising. There's loads of information out there about *what* to eat and *how* to exercise. There is no shortage of good information. We just can't seem to get ourselves to *do* it! Lack of motivation, focus or commitment is usually the true source of the problem. Coaching is often the only setting where men can openly deal with these kinds of challenges. It's perceptions, emotions and bad habits that get in the way of success. I see dramatic

change when clients learn to effectively master emotions, perceptions and focus. Learning to productively channel emotion is not more important for women than for men. It's important for everyone!

Tony:
Having sold for and served the financial services industry for many years, I can tell you men are definitely influenced by emotions when it comes to investing and investment decision making. In my experience, both with choosing investments and working with many male financial advisors, men tend to be highly competitive and more ego-driven. We want to win! Generally speaking, we go for investments that look like a winner, ignoring or dismissing valuable but less exciting opportunities. Men like home runs! We are also greatly influenced by success. The impression of power is intoxicating to us. If someone successful and powerful recommends an investment, men tend to follow the alpha male. That is not to say that we ignore data and automatically follow the drum-beat of the tribal chief, but we are influenced by emotional factors like winning, power and achievement. Men are not less emotion-driven investors than women; but they may be differently emotion-driven than women. In either case, emotion is the investor's worse enemy—man or woman. It's important to remember we must harness emotions for optimum performance.

The myth that women are irrational and frivolous with money is further dispelled when we look at the facts about how women spend money. The Bureau of Labor Statistics gathers information on American consumers. The data shows how much Americans spend on non-essential consumables like entertainment, alcohol, dining, audio/visual electronics, clothes, personal care items, etc. We promised not to overwhelm you with detail, so we'll not list all the statistics. The bottom line is that men spend about one quarter of their income on personal luxuries. Women are considerably less indulgent, spending about only one sixth of their income on extras.

Some skeptical readers may believe this data does not reveal the total picture. For example, married women frequently shop for the whole family. It might appear that their personal spending could be masked under family shopping statistics. However, that impression does not hold up under scrutiny. The data focuses on individual buyers with individual income, purchasing individual items, and does not reflect family purchasing.

In fact, we fully expect some readers to remain skeptical throughout. Skepticism is often an honest reaction based on personal history. We all carry biases based on our experiences. These are tenacious and hard to shake. The psychological phenomenon of *confirmation bias* leads us to notice behaviors that confirm existing expectations and to ignore evidence that contradicts our beliefs. During college, I (Barbara) spent a summer in France and lived with a French family. At that time, re-runs of the television show *Dallas* were playing on French TV. The host family watched *Dallas* religiously and was utterly convinced that all Americans lived *Dallas* style. Their experience hosting real American students (which they did regularly) could not dislodge this fixed expectation. I think their beliefs about the greedy, outrageous American characters portrayed in *Dallas* were more satisfying than the real Americans in their home. They ignored the humble existence of cash-strapped college students and preferred to focus on the images of splendorous wealth displayed on television. *Dallas* met their expectations far better than real students. We all need to be aware of our individual *confirmation biases* when working with others, male or female.

Similarly, our society is still overcoming *confirmation bias* about the role of women in commerce. Not long ago, women were minor players in the marketplace. Outdated impressions of women--such as those represented in television shows like *Leave it to Beaver* and *Father Knows Best*--still linger. There are good reasons why people have not focused on women clients. Women have been quietly growing in economic power while myths and stereotypes have concealed their increasing financial clout.

Our goal is to help you move past myths and outdated expectations. We want you to take hold of the great opportunity waiting for you and for women clients. Now, let's look at the current powerful reality of women and money!

Reality: Today's Woman Is America's Purchasing Manager

In reality, today's woman is an economic powerhouse. American women spend **seven trillion dollars annually!** They buy and buy big! Women control the purchases of:

> ➤ 91% homes

> ➤ 92% vacations

> ➤ 60% cars

> ➤ 55 billion dollars in consumer electronics

As we alluded to before, women control 85% of **all** purchases. Women are in charge of purchasing, but they're also much more!

Reality: Today's Woman Is the Financial Director at Home and Work

As a professional, you want clients who are financial directors as well as purchasing agents. Not to worry, women exercise great authority over family and business money. In fact, women assume the role of chief financial officer in most families. In addition, they are major powerhouses in the marketplace. Consider the following facts about women in the household:

$ Women control an estimated $14 trillion in assets, over 50% of all private wealth.

$ Women handle the money in 85% of families.

$ Half of all investors are women.

$ Women represent 39% of taxpayers classified as "top wealth holders".

$ Women head 45% of households with $600,000 or more in assets.

$ By 2012 women are expected to control two-thirds of all the private wealth.

$ 80-90% of women will be solely responsible for managing their own finances at some point in their lives.

Women not only direct the money at home, they're also increasingly influential in the marketplace. Below are the significant ways women control business dollars:

$ Women launch 70% of all businesses today.

$ 60% of women are employed outside the home.

$ In 40% of American companies, women hold 50% ownership.

$ Women own 10.6 million businesses.

$ The net worth of these owners range from 1-25 million dollars.

$ Women-owned businesses generate 2.6 trillion dollars in sales.

Clearly, women have money and are directing the finances both at home and in the workplace. They are valuable customers!

This largely untapped market is there for you to develop. The challenge is to focus your sights and seize the opportunity. In the remaining chapters we will get straight to work on helping you win new clients. First, we wanted to energize you for the challenge ahead. The opportunity is out there and it is huge!

Live on the Street

Yes, She Is Worth It!

In my travels with Claymore Securities I (Tony) meet many advisors. This led to our connection with David Hellinger and his partner Russ Emrath at Ameriprise Financial. When we learned of their focus on women clients we had to hear more. This is what David shared with us:

David worked with a variety of clients for a number of years, but around 2005 he began to reflect on the value of women clients. This was prompted by a workshop he attended about reaching women customers and David's annual discipline of strategic planning. During this period David discovered he already had a good number of single women clients, about 25% of his practice. He had fewer single men clients, about 10%. The remaining 65% of his practice were married couples. Upon further reflection, he realized in most of the couples, the wives were the prime decision makers. Also, these women were in regular contact with him. Suddenly it was clear that David already had strong client relationships with women across almost 90% of his practice. This was a foundation of success he could build on.

Determined to test the idea of specifically connecting with women, David asked his top women clients for input. All of the women were encouraging. In fact, they proactively connected him to more women and helped him grow. This trial period was so successful he decided to build a niche with this clear brand statement: "I work with successful women and their families to help them reach their important financial goals." In addition he developed a clear strategy that guides his marketing interactions. The response has been tremendous. He is routinely connected to women client prospects. David and his partner, Russ, are now focused on building their successful niche with women clients.

We asked David to share about his experiences. Here is what David told us:

Are there differences in selling to men clients vs. women clients?

Yes. If you establish a trusting relationship, women tend to appreciate a communicative and consultative approach. I find that women don't make the conversation a competition to see who is best or right. The tendency of men to be more competitive can get in the way of the working relationship with male clients. I find women easier to work with because we can have a cooperative dialogue about reaching their goals. Once I realized this, it was easy for me to build a trust relationship with women.

Are there any other differences in men and women clients?

Yes. Men can have a tendency to be more linear in their thinking. They tend to want checklists and focus on a to-do list. Women are generally more global in their thinking. They understand the big picture of their financial plan as part of their whole life. This works very well with my practice which takes comprehensive approach to financial planning. Women are also very faithful clients. They do what they say they'll do.

How have women clients impacted your growth?

I get many more referrals from women, 4 to 6 times more referrals then I get from male clients. I may get extra help because I have clearly stated my focus on women clients. Regardless, I find that women communicate more and tend to be more willing to share their good experience with other women. They also actively support my success beyond referrals. They genuinely want me to succeed.

How have your women advocates helped you?

They help me many ways! They give me good ideas and tell me what is appealing to women. For example, I have one client who is an accomplished business woman. Early on, she affirmed my style of relating, which was very helpful. She was very forthright in sharing the bad experiences she's had in the business world (not just the financial world). Though she is highly accomplished, many men are condescending. They wrongly assume she is uneducated in the ways of business. One of the reasons she became a client is that I did not patronize her. Frankly I was stunned, it never occurred to me to treat this very accomplished woman dismissively! That was great confirmation that my natural approach is truly respectful.

Are there any downsides?

Women clients have high expectations of service. I am a full service financial planner and they know that. They'll call me and want my input on every aspect of their financial life. I recently had a client call for my input on a home refinance. They reach out to me and want my input. I need to deliver!

Considering the high expectations, is it worth it?

Absolutely! If advisors don't realize they're worth it, then they really don't get it! That's OK with me. I'll be happy to take the women clients that they pass up. I prefer to work with women. I have very strong relationships with my clients. I find women easy to work with; they don't play games and they're open about what they need. They don't pretend to know things that they don't. Our relationships are warm and productive.

The Bottom Line

✓ There are 115 million adult women in the U.S. If your practice targets mostly men or male decision-makers, you're missing a large client market.

✓ There is a reason women are underserved. Cultural myths and outmoded expectations have left women unrecognized as major financial players. Savvy financial professionals will work to win this valuable customer.

✓ You have opportunity to access the seven trillion dollars that women disburse into the U.S. economy. Women control all major purchases in the household and increasingly in the workplace.

✓ Women control half the nation's wealth, $14 trillion in assets. By 2012 women are expected to control two-thirds of the private wealth in America. Now is the time for you to develop a focused and skilled strategy to capture this growing and significant client group.

The winner will be the professional who proves trustworthy to be involved with her and her money!

Individual Application

Use the space below to note facts and thoughts particularly relevant for you

_____

_____

_____

_____

_____

_____

_____

_____

Call to Action

1. **Look at your practice.** Go back now and look at your Female Market Test. Analyze your practice and ask yourself probing questions. How do I stack up? Do I have enough single women clients? Have I built a strong client relationship with the married women? Grade yourself on how well you're doing with this major market.

2. **Analyze the scope of your local market for women clients.** Find out the depth of the women's market in your community and in your service niche. Business and commerce associations (national, state and local) can help inform you on the local market. The more you know, the more you will be motivated to go after it.

3. **Determine your ideal female client.** Depending on your focus and your community, the ideal client may be younger professional women or older women responsible for legacy wealth. Determine your ideal female client!

4. **Pursue resources.** Connect to women professionals and find out how to connect with potential female clients. Reach out to female peers. Women colleagues are a fount of information!

Personal Goals & Action Steps

Use the chart below to enter goals, action steps and target dates related to your goals

#1 Goal →	#2 Action Steps →	#3 Target Date

CHAPTER 2

How Much Do I Want Her?

Rapid Rundown

In the last chapter we uncovered the huge female market potential. There is plenty of opportunity out there. Opportunity is only one part of success. Equally important is strong motivation. This chapter helps evaluate your interest and increase your motivation to drive success.

Nut and Bolts

Am I Ready to Attract Women Clients?

Have you ever entered a female world and felt distinctly uncomfortable? Perhaps the first time you entered a lingerie store or stumbled into a bridal shower. It probably felt like a different world. Perhaps it was a bit uncomfortable. You had to want to be there to stay. Few men are eager to stay in such circumstances without strong incentive. Similarly, we're taking you to a place that may feel foreign. If you've had a pleasant taste of this world, great! That's reinforcement and encouragement to continue. For those who are not so familiar, we're here to help you become adept and comfortable in this new world. First, get ready for the journey. Strong incentive is vitally important. How much do you want go there? Your level of motivation is critical. Desire drives success. You must want it!

Step One. Want To!

Stories can be powerful examples. Recently, I (Barbara) was on vacation at an outstanding resort. While there, I struck up a conversation with a handsome and successful man in his mid-thirties. I'll call him "Curt." As an executive coach who is committed to helping people succeed, I enjoy listening to people wherever I am. In turn, people tell me their stories. Soon, I discovered Curt had once dated the perfect woman. She was everything he wanted and more! Sadly, while she was within his grasp, he was reluctant to seal the deal. Like many, he took the easy road. He thought he could enjoy the benefits of her affection without committing. While she eagerly waited, he hesitated. Ultimately she grew discouraged with his lack of commitment. She left and married another man. Though it's been ten years, he deeply regrets losing her! Curt lost the opportunity of his life because he just didn't *want* her enough to seal the deal. She figured that out and went elsewhere. You're in the same position as Curt, want it enough and you'll be motivated to succeed. If you don't, you won't.

How Do I Want To?

Your desire will increase by focusing on the great opportunity with women clients. To reinforce your interest we'll reiterate some key motivators:

➤ Women will control two-thirds of all private wealth by 2012. They already control half now. There is a huge opportunity in the hands of women.

➤ 80-90% of women will be the sole directors of their money at some point. If you don't connect with these women, someone else will be managing their funds.

➤ 70% of all new businesses are started by women. Working well with women will become increasingly important as they direct more and more business dollars.

In addition, according to national IRS data:

➤ There is a large group of wealthy prospects. Over one million women have a net worth of at least one million dollars.

➤ Women represent 43% of *all* Americans with over $500,000 in investable assets. That's a huge volume of client assets.

Furthermore, according to independent surveys:

➤ 53% of high-wealth women (three million dollars in investable assets and net worth over eight million dollars) <u>earned</u> their money working. Most wealthy women are not passive beneficiaries.

➤ In half of all affluent couples ($500,000 of investable assets), both work full time. Most of these couples made <u>joint</u> financial decisions.

➤ Only 21% of affluent couples have a stay-at-home spouse. Clearly most women are engaged in the marketplace.

Not only are women quality client prospects, but women need the benefit of sound financial guidance:

➤ Women spend more time out of the workforce attending to child-rearing and other family duties (12.6 *years* for women compared to only 10.4 *months* for men). Consequently, work-based retirement savings and social security benefits may be much smaller than male peers.

➤ 75% of caretakers for elderly family members are women, negatively impacting working time and earning power.

➤ The average age of widowhood is 56. Female life expectancy is now age 81. That's 25 years of single widowhood. Women need to be financially prepared!

Need is not the only incentive. Women continue to grow in earning power:

> Today there are 33% more female college graduates than male graduates.

> Women earn half of all the law degrees and medical degrees.

> Large women-owned businesses (over 500 employees) grew 125% in five years.

> 46% of all management and professional positions are now held by women.

These statistics are probably outdated by the printing of this book. That's how fast things are changing today. We completely expect the numbers are even greater as you read this. As women gain more professional stature their income will grow, as will their need for quality financial services.

Barbara & Tony Speak Out!

The need for education and access to quality professional services is evident when you turn on the television or radio. First, ask financial advisors what they think of pop culture money celebrities. Then ask psychologists what they think of talk show therapists and you'll likely get a similar response from both groups of professionals: "They're awful!"

Barbara:
I've never met a financial advisor who endorsed the money pop-slop that is spewed across the airways. I've had good education on the value of quality financial guidance. Similarly, if my clients ask me about celebrity pop therapists, I have an equally strong aversion. Just like financial security is not achieved in cute sound bites, neither is quality counseling!

Equally, I dislike businesses that peddle generic advice and cookie-cutter programs and call it coaching and training. Individualized coaching and custom team development are superior and distinctive. Just as your service is completely different from those financial hawkers that make you cringe, an off-the-shelf product cannot be compared to professional coaching!

Tony:
Similarly, thirty-second investment advice is frequently worthless and recently been proved to be dangerous. Yet it persists! There is no value in pop finance and quick tips. However, if real wisdom and good information is not accessible, intelligent people will follow any available advice. If we don't reach out with our expertise, they have no other choice. The need to provide vital knowledge and wise guidance is great. After all, financial professionals are not just mouthpieces hired to entertain and fill air space. You have the tremendous opportunity to help build individual and generational wealth. It is a high calling and valuable service!

Client interest is just as important as need and opportunity. Today more than ever, women want financial services support!

$ 67% of women have retirement investments.

$ 61% of high-wealth women want to be involved in managing their money.

$ 56% of women are interested in gaining wealth.

$ 78% of women are pursuing financial/retirement goals.

With nearly 80% of women pursuing financial goals, they are clearly focused on the management of their money.

Motivation Self-Assessment

Strong motivation is essential to success. It is important for you to measure your level of this critical factor. Take a moment to get a snapshot or your interest. Read the statements below. Make a check mark by the one that best fits your thoughts right now.

1. _____ *I really don't want to change my business practice. I am successful and I don't need to attract any more clients—women or men.*

2. _____ *I think I should want to develop more female clients, but I like the way I do things now. I have a good system for me. New skills or techniques don't really interest me.*

3. _____ *I want to attract more female investor clients, but I hesitate to start anything new. I am very comfortable with the way I attract, retain and serve all my clients.*

4. _____ *I have tried attracting women clients, but have been frustrated by it. I am not sure I want to try again. It may not be worth it.*

5. _____ *I just don't know how I feel or what I think right now.*

6. _____ *I want to attract more female investor clients and I am willing to consider ideas and skills that would make me more successful. If the ideas look good to me, I will give it a sincere try.*

7. _____ *I cannot ignore the female-investor client any longer. I am completely willing to adapt my habits to be more successful with women clients.*

8. _____ *I came to this book already interested in attracting more female investor clients. I am willing and motivated (and may have completed some goals already).*

9. _____ *I have worked at attracting women clients and have succeeded. I want to do more to achieve higher success.*

Motivation Score

✓ Agreed with statements 1, 2, 3 or 4 = Very Weak to Weak Motivation

✓ Agreed with statements 6, 7, 8 or 9 = Strong to Very Strong Motivation

✓ Agreed with statement 5 = Undecided

For those readers who have weak motivation, we suggest you read through this book and do some field testing. Test the waters in any way that might impact your interest. Below are some field test suggestions:

➤ Ask female financial advisors about the topic. We're confident you'll hear plenty of incentives from women professionals.

➤ Evaluate your market. Can you afford to ignore the women in your community? Do you have enough clients to sustain and grow your practice by focusing on men alone? What about the women in your couple clients? Will they stay with you if their husbands are out of the picture? Are you sure?

➤ Ask women consumers who will speak frankly. Ask them:
  o How well does the financial services industry help them?
  o Do they feel comfortable seeking help from financial services professionals?
  o Are they pleased with how their advisors have served them?

We're confident that those with low motivation will find abundant entice-
ment. We want your motivation to be as high as possible. It will greatly
enhance success. For those readers who are frankly undecided, we suggest
you follow the same route as those with lower motivation. Keep reading
and do some field testing, it will help you decide. For those readers who are
well motivated, great! Strong motivation is vital.

Field Test Tools

Barbara:
There is a powerful exercise used in coaching to sort out facts and
motivation. You can try it for yourself. This takes a bit of time, but it
is tremendously powerful as a motivation clarifier and booster. Follow
the steps in order:

Step 1: List all the negatives (-) of **working** to gain more women
clients.
Step 2: List all the positives (+) of **not working** to gain more women
clients.
Step 3: List all the negatives (-) of **not gaining** more women clients.
Step 4: List all the positives (+) of **gaining** more women clients.

Now compare the lists. It's human nature for people to focus on
avoiding immediate pain and gaining immediate pleasure. Any time
we consider a change, it's hard for us to move past these immediate
issues. The above process allows you to consider the total picture of
all positives and negatives. It also helps us to look at the short-term
and long-term consequences of our impulses. The size and quality of
your lists will be your deciding factor. If the lists for steps 3 and 4
are longer and/or display more important factors than those for steps 1
and 2, your decision is made. Working to gain women clients is well
worth your time and effort.

> **Tony:**
> As an alternative, consider whether your practice has reached its peak
> level. If not, why not? For many of us change is difficult. Few invite
> it. In my experience, when you embrace change, good things happen.
> If your practice is fine and you are busy (with productive work), and
> have the life you want, then you may not need to innovate. However, if
> you've picked up this book interested in growing; good for you. Read
> on! Use all available resources to support your growth.

The Power of a Value Statement

After you're initially motivated, your next objective is to keep motivation
strong as you develop expertise in working with women clients. New
initiatives take persistence to execute. It's normal to experience temporary
dips in drive. To prevent distraction and discouragement, we encourage you to summarize your female client development goal into a value
statement. The purpose is to summarize and reinforce important benefits
that reaching the goal will provide. Short, but powerful works best. An
example might be:

> *"I want to skillfully increase my number of female investors because broadening
> my client base gives me_____."*

Then, list the core benefits, such as:

1. *Cutting edge service*
2. *Profitable practice*
3. *Unique niche/brand*
4. *Professional success*
5. _____ (Any motivator that is true for you.)

She Said/He Said:
The Power of Keeping Motivation Strong

Barbara:

Boosting motivation is a regular part of coaching. I frequently initiate a value statement exercise similar to our previous suggestion. Even though everybody struggles with keeping up momentum, people are less than enthusiastic when presented with this exercise. Reluctance and skepticism are common. If you're skeptical of the value statement exercise, I understand. Most clients react the same way. After clients express their doubt, I suggest they give it a try and we go through specific steps. I also promise that we'll throw the whole idea out if it fails. Clients then complete the exercise on their own in between meetings. Guaranteed, they come to next coaching session utterly amazed and transformed. Every client who conscientiously completes this technique reports dramatic results! Focus and drive are critical to reaping the fabulous reward of a practice full of female investor clients. You are the primary source of your success!

Tony:

During my career, focusing on motivation and being willing to change has worked well. At two important points in my career, I made "risky" changes. On one occasion, I requested a job change that caused me to give up some control and organizational power. I gave up an entire department that produced revenue, with hundreds of employees reporting to me. I did this to pursue something that only a few key supporters and I believed would be a tremendous value to the firm. I also believed it would bring me great personal satisfaction. Others were less enthusiastic. Some senior executives asked if I was "OK", out of concern for my future. At another point of opportunity, I "gave up" significant financial security for increased flexibility, which provided me tremendous growth. Both were risky choices and both paid off on all fronts. In order to pursue opportunities, I had to embrace change and focus my motivation, while releasing familiar roles and comfortable routines. I encourage you to consider seizing opportunity to bring great transformation.

The key is to find the drivers that are **most important for you.** These core motivators will keep you going when your attention is distracted or energy temporarily wanes. We encourage you to write them down and keep them visible.

Our goal is to build an equation for your success in attracting, retaining and serving female investor clients. The first step is to decide if she is worth it, our focus for chapter one. The second step is to determine how much you want and need her, our current chapter topic. Now we can move on to the skills that will transform your interest and motivation into a reality, becoming a desirable and successful service professional for women clients!

Live on the Street

The High Value of Women Clients

Ernest Dorsey has 18 years of experience in financial services. He has worked in many facets of the industry including time as a specialist and member on the Midwest Stock Exchange (now the Chicago Stock Exchange). As an institutional trader for a brokerage firm in Chicago, he bought and sold millions of shares a day for large mutual and pension funds. In addition, Ernest launched and ran the Chicago office of an Atlanta based investment banking firm. During the first year of operation, he participated in over one billion dollars in bond issues. Ernest is currently a financial advisor with one of the largest and most successful securities firms in the industry. Recently Ernest told us his story of working with female investor clients. It's tremendous!

Tell us about how you started this focus on female investors?

My mother is a career nurse in contact with many physicians (mostly male). I asked for her assistance in connecting with these professionals. Her response was helpful, but also a direct challenge.

What did she say?

She was very blunt. I remember it well. She said: "You need to talk with my peers, the ladies. You guys come around all the time and walk right past us. We've got money and no one pays any attention to us."

I listened. Right then and there, I decided to focus more on women clients. Rather than bother my family, I contacted a female pharmacist friend and started networking.

What did you do to connect with women prospects?

I started conducting marketing events for women professionals. The first few were typical advisor workshops.

What do you mean by typical advisor workshops?

I gave them food and I talked. The result of these first events was merely mediocre. Then, I decided to focus more specifically on what women might appreciate. I conducted two exclusive workshops for women professionals, set at a spa with extra benefits, like wine tastings and manicures.

How did the women-focused events work out?

The response was tremendous! As a result of the workshops, I was invited to speak at several professional meetings reaching a total of 150 people. I had an outstanding response to this exposure: 30% became prospective clients. I had a conversion rate of 80% from prospects to active clients. This all came from being invited to only two speaking engagements by female client advocates. I don't think most marketing efforts deliver a hot prospect rate of 30% and an 80% rate of converting prospects to clients.

Do you find there are differences in working with male and female clients?

Yes, I find distinctive patterns in selling to men and selling to women.

Would you share these differences?

This is what I found when selling to men:

> ➢ Male prospects frequently used our conversation to boast about their stock market knowledge or latest day trading profits. Many were more interested in looking impressive, than becoming clients.

> ➢ The sales approach with men is very different. Men need charts and graphs. They also expect an expert. A persuasive presentation is important when selling to men.

> If I spent time persuading married men, they would then leave to confer with their wives. Too often prospects were lost at this stage. Most men would not return if their wives had any hesitation. I lost too many prospects this way.

This is what I found in selling to women:

> I learned immediately to shut-up and listen. I need to allow them to talk, ask questions and share their stories.

> Also, I learned that women take longer to process and decide. They need to visit and revisit the idea until they become comfortable. It helped me adapt when I remembered how my mother shopped during my childhood. She would shop around several stores and even go back to some before she decided. It doesn't bother me now, because I know that this is how many women make decisions.

> Lastly, I learned that once a married woman is convinced, the deal is done. She brings her husband in when it's time to sign the papers. Rarely does a husband question his wife's due diligence in finding a quality professional.

Is it worth it?

> **Yes!** Women tell me what they are thinking. I don't have to guess.

> **Yes!** Women give me referrals proactively and voluntarily. They even call me back later to add more names to the referral list.

> **Yes!** Women do my marketing for me. They call and invite me to events as an expert speaker and I get great exposure and response from these invitations!

The Bottom Line

✓ Strong motivation is critical to success. You need to want it!

✓ Focusing and boosting interest is important for execution and success.

✓ We are building an achievement formula:

Value *(She is worth it)* + Motivation *(You want her)* + Skill = Success

Individual Application

Use the space below to note facts and thoughts particularly relevant for you.

_____

_____

_____

_____

_____

_____

_____

_____

_____

Call to Action

1. **Recall success.** Remember other times in your life when taking a risk or learning a new skill paid off. Changing old habits is challenging. Remembering when risk brought rewards will increase your openness to new ideas. Recalling times when working toward a goal brought you success will refuel your energy for new challenges. It's most powerful if you make it more tangible by discussing it and writing it down.

2. **Find motivators.** Identify core motivators for developing more female investor clients. What benefits are most important for you? Develop a value statement that gives you a clear reminder of your goal and the benefits of reaching the goal.

3. **Increase interest.** If your motivation is less than strong, field test the value of the new client business. Anything you can do to increase your interest will benefit you now and in the future.

Personal Goals & Action Steps

Use the chart below to enter goals, action steps and target dates related to your goals

#1 Goal	→	#2 Action Steps	→	#3 Target Date

CHAPTER 3

Connecting With Her

This chapter describes broad differences in how men and women relate. It highlights the need to shift perspective and focus in order to successfully develop more women clients.

Nuts and Bolts

Connecting vs. Winning

Let's begin winning some of the $14 trillion in assets women control. That's probably what you've been waiting for all along. "Just hurry up and tell me how to win the assets of women clients" might be your gut response about now. We're going to start right now! **The first thing we need to do is move away from the concept of winning.** In the previous chapter, we focused on the importance of you *wanting* to work within a women's world. Now, it is our job to help you *enter that world comfortably*. Part of that is helping you understand what's important to women clients. We need to use concepts that help you appreciate their viewpoint. The language we use reinforces the core ideas and guides how you will execute the skills. Don't worry we won't spend all our time on a discussion of concepts. We will also outline concrete steps. Frankly, that's the easy part! The more difficult skill involves you learning how to communicate well and work skillfully within the female culture. Consequently, we're doing everything we can to facilitate your journey into the world of female clients, hence the title: *Connecting With Her.*

The concept of "connecting" with others is not new, but it's receiving renewed attention and support. In his book, *Blink* (Little Brown & Co., 2005), Malcolm Gladwell explored why some physicians get sued for malpractice, while others do not. Gladwell found that doctors with a superior bedside manner were less likely to be sued, *regardless of the actual quality of care*. Having conversations to connect with the patient (which took only three more minutes) made all the difference in the patient's perception of the doctor. Only **three minutes** focused on connecting resulted in satisfied patients. Conversely, doctors who didn't spend a few moments to connect suffered higher rates of malpractice. Clearly, focusing on connection matters. It's also important to note that the successful doctors had a *superior* bedside manner. Not only did they spend time connecting, they also did it well. We want the same for you, a strong connection focus and superior skill.

Barbara & Tony's Advice for the Journey: Adapt!

Travel experiences are good examples of how to adapt. I (Tony) recently enjoyed a trip to Italy and I (Barbara) went to London. While comparing travel stories, we noticed how much easier it is to visit a country with a language and culture similar to our own. When traveling in Italy, communication can be difficult. Conversely, visiting London is easy for Americans, since we share a common heritage and language. Yet, we are more comfortable and effective when we adapt. In London you need to translate a few menu items into American terms. *Bangors* are sausages, *gammon* is ham and *biscuits* are cookies. It's also helpful to adopt local courtesies to avoid unnecessary offense. For example, all Londoners stand single file, to the right, on escalators. It's *extremely* rude to block the left-hand side of the aisle. In the U.S. people stand all over the place on public escalators. It's just not part of our national habit to keep an open passing lane (although we think this would be great courtesy to start in our country!).

Fortunately, interacting with women clients is not like traveling to Italy. It's more like visiting London. We have common roots, a common language, and an understanding of the basic culture. It's new, but familiar. Be confident that, if you shift your language to align with the dialect and adapt your habits to local courtesies, you will be comfortable and welcome.

Let's move on to connecting with her! That's the fundamental idea and it's different from winning or attracting her. When you attract something you focus on how you look, your image, your presentation. In the animal world, the male of the species attracts by showing great strength, bright plumage or overt dominance. In the human culture it's usually the women who put on the bright plumage to attract attention. In either case, it's a great show! The focus is on the presentation. That's the emphasis when you think of "attracting". When you connect with someone, the focus is on the other person. They are in the spotlight, not you. Your goal is to find out about them and draw them out. You spend less time *presenting yourself* and more time *seeking their input*. You work to make them comfortable and build relationship. **Your entire attitude is different.**

It's critical that you make this shift in perspective. You can execute all the tactical steps brilliantly and still fail. If you're more focused on making a great show than on building genuine connection, you risk appearing fake. Phony connection will not bring you lasting success! What's more, women are usually highly intuitive about relationships. If a woman gets a hint that you're insincere, it's all over!

Connection is Key

Most men and women connect differently. Men's relationships tend to be task-focused and independent. They frequently connect around an activity or event. Communicating to create a personal bond is usually not the focus. When they do communicate the interaction tends to be more competitive than cooperative. Even the best of friends will enjoy exchanging taunts. Friendly verbal sparring is the norm.

Women do just the opposite. Women are generally relationship focused and cooperative. They connect by talking and sharing personal stories. As they interact they work to stay on an equal plane. In fact, women will often play down their own accomplishments in order to make other women feel more comfortable. Just listen to women give each other compliments. The compliment receiver usually lowers her own status by a self-deprecating, "It was nothing" type of response or raises the other woman's status by giving her a compliment in return. This brings the women back onto an equal level.

Remember these social scenarios when you work with women. Most men work competitively. They tend to naturally form a hierarchy. Someone is the alpha male and every other man has to find his place in a vertical order. They intuitively compete for a higher level as they interact together. This is all natural and expected. No one talks about it, it just happens. A totem pole is a good image for male hierarchical interactions. Reaching the top of the totem pole is every man's goal. Conversely, most women work cooperatively. Women try to stay on the same level. Women prefer a horizontal and circular world. A round conference table is a good illustration for women's cooperative, equality-focused style.

That being said, it's important we highlight equal value across genders. A competitive or cooperative relationship style is not better or worse; it's just different. We also need to remember that not every man and every woman fits the general tendency. There are men who are highly cooperative and relationship focused and women who are not. Our goal is to make you aware of these general patterns, so you can have more insight into your own natural style and the styles of those around you. Take note of how the men in your environment relate. Also, note how the women tend to relate. The pattern will probably generally fit and, of course, there will be exceptions. It is important that you notice your own approach and become more adaptable to the perspective around you. If you find that the women around you and many women clients tend to have a cooperative style, its important for you to shift to their perspective.

She Said/He Said:
Men and Women's Differences

Barbara:

I think stories bring home the reality of fundamental differences between men and women. My husband and I have three sons. One Christmas vacation we went to northern Wisconsin for a week of fun in the snow. My eldest brought a friend. Our younger sons are twins. So my husband and I travelled with four teenage boys: two 17 year-olds and two 14 year-olds. There were five males and me. One day, during a late leisurely brunch around the dining table, I decided to experiment with conversation. What would happen if I didn't *initiate* conversation, like I usually do? I tried my experiment and what ensued was astonishing. During that long brunch, utter silence. Not one word was spoken! All five men sat around contentedly eating without speaking a word to each other. I sat there stunned. It took all my self-control not to break the deafening silence. When I joked about it later, they all stared at me bewildered. This was perfectly normal and actually quite nice for them. They just wanted to eat. Let me tell you, this would **never** happen with a group of females. If it did, it would be a sign of a serious problem in the relationships. It's been quite an education for me, raised in a house full of girls to raise a house full of sons. I have learned to appreciate different, but valuable, things about boys as I have watched my sons and their friends. In particular, boys have an easy way of moving past disagreements. They work it out quickly and move on. It's delightful!

Tony:

This winter I was sitting at a restaurant in a ski lodge in the Midwest, looking out over the slopes as my son and four other 14-year old boys spent the day snowboarding. It was a great day for them and a great time for me. I sat at a table alone with my Blackberry was enjoying some quiet, productive time. Then, I saw, at the next table, a woman commandeering seven 11-year old boys.

All seven boys had come in from the slopes to have lunch with this woman, who was clearly the mother of one boy. As I watched them, I was reminded of the differences between genders. First, I noticed her gift at managing this group of energetic boys. I was glad the high school freshmen I was chaperoning were far more interested in the slopes than me. She mastered crowd control, created fun and had those young kids under wraps for nearly two hours. I'm sure the same thing would not have happened if I had been in control. Second, I was reminded of my 11-year-old daughter and how radically different it would be if this group had been a gathering of girls. There is no doubt that men are different from women—even at a young age. This is a good thing. Embrace it. Frequently, women are more competent in areas of organization, event planning, attending to details, etc. I am glad we're made differently. We need to celebrate and enjoy working with the talents each brings to our world.

How Do I Shift Perspective?

If you are used to managing clients and directing the sales/service process, then this is a big shift. If you tend to adapt yourself to your client's interests and personalize your approach to each person, the shift will be easier. The first step in shifting perspective is to examine your main goal as you interact with each potential client.

Set Your Main Goal

What are you after? What are you *thinking and pursuing* when attracting clients? Below are some examples of what advisors might be thinking (in terms of goals) when attracting clients:

> ➤ *I want to build my business! This client would be a valuable step in reaching that goal.*

> ➢ *This is a person of influence. If I could win this client, I will gain many referrals.*

> ➢ *I would love to manage this client's assets. It would be a welcome challenge.*

> ➢ *This client would be a trouble-free client. I would gain great benefit without big hassle.*

> ➢ *This client fits well into my business niche. We are a good match!*

What do you notice about these very reasonable goals? They're all about what the client will give you and what you will gain from the client. The focus is on the object of the goal: larger business, referrals, good challenge, reward with ease, compatibility with your practice. We're not criticizing these types of goals. After all, this is a business relationship. In business, people are supposed to bring a benefit to the business partnership. You scratch my back and I'll scratch yours. There is absolutely nothing wrong with wanting positive objective benefits from clients! We are in business to profit; it's not a charitable service. However, with women, you are on dangerous ground if gaining the **object** is your first goal. It will set your perspective and affect how you treat women clients; and it's risky. For men, it is acceptable to want to win and gain a prize. Winning is expected and respected! What man does not admire the top producer in his profession (even grudgingly)? For women the most important goal is: **Relationship.**

We are covering a lot of material in this book. Sometimes it can be challenging to remember everything, especially if it is new. When I (Barbara) run workshops that are dense with content, I have a practice to help participants. That practice is to highlight key things to remember along the way. I usually precede this by saying: "If you only take away one thing from this section remember *"remember this..."*. That was the impetus for the **Bottom Line** section at the end of each chapter and the space to make notes that are significant for you. We want you to be able to retain the important things as you move forward. We have now reached the cornerstone of this entire topic right here. There is one ultimate bottom line. If you remember only one concept out of this entire book, we are asking you to remember always:

1. Your first goal is to build a strong relationship!

2. Your second goal is to never forget about the relationship!

3. Your third goal is to keep the relationship in mind as you do all the other important things!

Word of Caution: *We are absolutely confident in everything we assert in this book. However, we want to repeat the warning from our introduction (especially for those readers who routinely skip introductions). Traditional stereotypes of women are frequently inaccurate and we spend considerable space debunking these myths. At the same time, we must acknowledge that all generalizations are dangerous--even the well-researched generalizations we are reporting. We are utilizing this data to help you recognize overall patterns and raise your awareness. However, our purpose is to increase your flexibility, not create new stereotypes. Obviously, not all women are the same. We encourage you to genuinely listen, learn and be open to what is important to each client and prospect.*

Live on the Street

The Power of Connection

We're tremendously grateful to the advisors who've shared their experiences with us. There is great power in seeing dry data come to life in the real-life successes of financial advisors. We were excited to hear the story of Jodi Manthei from Riverstone Wealth Partners. Her account is so perfectly matched with our premise that it's astonishing. When we approached Jodi, we told her that we were writing a book about women investor clients and we heard she had success with a recent woman-to-woman event. Then we asked her to tell us about her practice. Here is what she shared:

Jodi started an independent financial services practice last year. She spent many years in the investment department of a regional bank which was recently purchased by a large national entity. Jodi decided that the new organization was not a good fit. She started fresh as an independent advisor and launched Riverstone Wealth Partners, leaving her bank clients behind as required. She became a registered representative of INVEST Financial Corporation, member FINRA, SIPC. As a registered investment advisor, Jodi offers securities and advisory services through INVEST Financial. We asked her to share about her new practice. Here is what she told us:

Tell me about your practice. Do you have a focus?

I guess my focus could be called "generational". I have lots of multi-generational clients that include many family members: parents, children, siblings, nieces, nephews etc... Client's extended families have a lot do to with their financial interests. In the process of developing financial plans I become aware of other family members, who often become clients as well. The generational client base is more a result of the referrals I get, than an intentional focus.

How did you get your new practice started?

95% of my clients from the bank came and *found me* within the first three months. I was very fortunate.

Your clients had no idea where you were—really?

I've seen bad repercussions happen to advisors who tried to get around the "no contact" rule. I was very cautious. My clients had no advance knowledge that I was leaving the bank, nor did they know where I went.

How did they find you?

They did some detective work on their own. A few had personal contact information. Once one client knew where I was, they passed along the information and the clients called me.

What do you think most male advisors do that might be different from your approach?

I think many male advisors miss the connection piece of the client relationship. They don't take enough time to deepen the relationship or just listen to the client share about their life and their needs. Most clients have layers to their lives. Much comes out when you get beyond the first layer. I think there is a fundamental need to be understood. When we spend time to genuinely understand clients we earn their trust.

Do you think going below the surface changes your financial advice or plan?

Not necessarily, but you may uncover needs or concerns that impact your recommendations. You can do a good investment plan without deep understanding. But if you don't understand the client, you just have a customer. When you spend time to develop connection and relationship, you are much more likely to have a loyal client. You also have a client who becomes an active advocate!

Speaking of advocates, how do you get referrals for the family and friends that come to you?

You know every advisor is supposed to have a system for requesting referrals. (I just went to a seminar on that.) I attribute my success more to being lucky, since many of my clients send people to me voluntarily. I make a point of thanking them with a call, a note and usually a small gift card. I confess, I don't do a particularly good job of asking for referrals. When I do ask, my clients often tell me that they just gave my name to someone.

Tell me about your client demographics?

Well, I have about a 50-50 split between men and women. I have many married couples. I have a good group of single women and single men too. I even have divorced clients who stayed with me individually, after the divorce.

What is different about selling to men clients vs. women clients?

I don't do anything different with my men and women clients. I focus on building connections and relationships with everyone. I find it works equally well for both men and women.

I understand you did a woman-to-woman event recently?

Yes, just recently. I partnered with two other professional women (a banker, a lawyer and me) to put together an event for 80 women attendees. It's too early to see the full impact, but the initial feedback was very enthusiastic.

What kind of feedback did you get?

Not only did the women really enjoy the event, but many participants requested to meet with one or all of us to pursue important life goals. We are planning follow up meetings and other similar events. It was a great success!

To summarize, you're successful because:

➢ You spend time building connection and relationship with clients. You learn about their lives and their family.

➢ From this connection you learn about what is important to them and build trust.

➢ You find these relationships build long-term loyal clients.

➢ In fact, your clients did detective work to pursue you after you left the bank.

➢ Your clients voluntarily send referrals.

➢ You treat men and women clients with the same focus on building connection.

➢ You find that both men and women become strongly loyal clients and advocates when you focus on building relationship.

Yes, I am very fortunate. I am grateful for my clients, their advocacy and the work we do together!

The Bottom Line

✓ Working with women requires adapting to a familiar, but new, culture.

✓ Women prefer to work cooperatively on an equal plane.

✓ Shift your perspective from an attraction focus to a connection focus.

✓ Always remember to build relationship.

Individual Application

Use the space below to note facts and thoughts particularly relevant for you

Call to Action

1. **Analyze biases.** Examine your openness to new viewpoints. Are you ready to adapt to a women's culture to be a successful connector with female investors and clients? Identify reasons to shift. List benefits and motivators.

2. **Evaluate your approach.** Are you more attraction or connection focused in your approach? If you are connection focused, is it a constant focus or just part of an initial sales process? Write down your habits during the sales and service process. Decide what (if anything) needs to shift.

3. **Shift focus.** How might you adjust your approach to women clients to enhance the equal partnership feeling? Establish goals and a strategy to connect well with women.

4. **Activate changes.** What can you do to activate the goal of building relationship as a primary focus? Set concrete actions steps with deadlines to keep you moving forward.

Personal Goals & Action Steps

Use the chart below to enter goals, action steps and target dates related to your goals

#1 → Goal	#2 Action Steps →	#3 Target Date

CHAPTER 4

Partnering With Her

Rapid Rundown

In this chapter we explain the sales-and-service model of working with female clients. We explain the whole process, including more details about connecting as you develop the new client relationship. This chapter is the longest in the book. We decided it was preferable to explain the entire model of working with women without breaking it into several chapters. This comprehensive approach also fits the way women operate. All these stages are part of one continuous professional relationship with women clients. Women tend to view things in terms of the whole relationship. It will help you if you do the same.

Nuts and Bolts

A Partnering Approach

Now that you have appealed to women clients through a connection focus, you're entering the stage of establishing the professional relationship. We typically encounter the business terms *landing* and *retaining* the client at this stage. These terms bring to mind the idea of *capturing* and *owning* the client—as if the client is an object for you to win. It sets the stage for a competitive approach. As we highlighted in the last chapter, men are frequently comfortable with a competitive approach. Women are generally not! Women usually relate in a cooperative, equality-based manner. This affects how you will work with them. For women clients, leave the competitive approach behind.

When working with women, focus on cooperative equal partnership. This does not diminish your expertise or your value. Women come to advisors because they need professional knowledge and services. You can be the expert and work cooperatively at the same time, in a peer relationship. You are not above them as a director, nor below them as a subordinate. Both the advisor and the client have equally important roles. The client is an expert in her life and what she wants financially. The financial professional is an expert on products and services to reach her goals.

Power of Partnership

Partnering with women clients is powerful for both the advisor and the client. We've already established the benefit of partnering for you. Women are financial heavyweights. Equally important, they need you! Women have substantial financial needs and they have been underserved for too long. You provide a tremendous opportunity to build their financial success. Reflect on the following statistics:

➤ Women have fewer employer-sponsored retirement plans.

➤ Women's income decreases 50% at the loss of a spouse.

➤ 47% of high-wealth women (net worth over eight million dollars) fear losing money.

➤ 64% of women are worried about their retirement savings.

➤ 83% of women are worried that inflation will overtake their retirement income.

➤ 74% of women are single when they pass away.

➤ If a woman reaches age 50 without cancer or heart disease, she can expect to reach age 92.

You have a great deal of expertise to offer women and they need it. **Less than half** of all women feel confident in their investment knowledge. Women know that they need your expertise. Research shows, women's confidence increases dramatically when they have a financial professional working with them. Consider this:

➤ 63% of women who have a financial advisor feel confident in their financial future.

➤ 66% of women who have a financial advisor feel knowledgeable about investing.

The positive impact of quality financial advice is clear. Less than half of those without an advisor feel confident. A full two-thirds with an advisor have a sense of confidence and knowledge. Your services are important and desperately needed. What's more, women clients know they need help. So why aren't women pounding down your door asking for your services? Why do we even need this book urging you to proactively reach out to them? We believe the disconnection between women and financial services is caused by two main sources. First, the myths and misinformation we detailed earlier. Second, the outdated and ineffective tactics used to attract female clients. For example, the traditional sales approach does not work well with women. This approach follows the following sales formula:

Present Offering + Highlight Benefits + Defeat Objections + Push for the "Yes" = Sale

Consumer research overwhelming confirms that women reject this approach. We believe the old-school sales formula is rooted in the competitive model that focuses on capturing the sale. Put on a good show and push for a commitment. It is all about showing attractiveness and winning. It has nothing to do with connection or partnering. It does not match a woman's way of relating. She doesn't want to be viewed as an object to be won or her money as a prize to be captured.

Even more, it does not match women's style of buying. In fact, it is so mismatched that a full third of women do not trust *any* salesperson—on principle! This research shows the competitive model of sales is not aligned with women's buying style. Here's how women buy:

➢ Consult their friends and people they know.

➢ Gather lots of information from many sources.

➢ Ask a lot of questions.

➢ Need/want time to consider.

When a woman tells a traditional sales person they need more information, the sales person will typically push to overcome the woman's hesitancy. They may interpret her hesitancy as stalling. If the woman then decides to think about it and revisit later, the traditional sales person will push harder for commitment. The salesman fears loss of the sale if the customer walks out the door. Unfortunately, this method actually drives women away from the sale. It communicates to the woman that the sales person is:

➢ **Not listening** to her.

➢ Wants to **win the sale** rather than help her.

➢ Is **not** willing to answer questions cooperatively, is **arguing** with her.

➢ Is **not** working **with** her, is **bulldozing** her.

If you've been frustrated when trying to land women clients, perhaps the approach was the core problem. Approaches that work with male clients often do not match a female client's interest. Prospects may be lost solely because of style. The key is to partner with (not capture) women clients.

How to Partner with Women

In the last chapter we discussed appealing to the female investor and introduced the basic premise of connecting with her. Our partnering model
extends and expands the idea of connection all the way through the client
relationship. We will begin with a graphic depiction of the model and then
explain each of the five areas: **Connect, Understand, Integrate, Co-Create**
and **Serve.**

Partnering with Women Clients

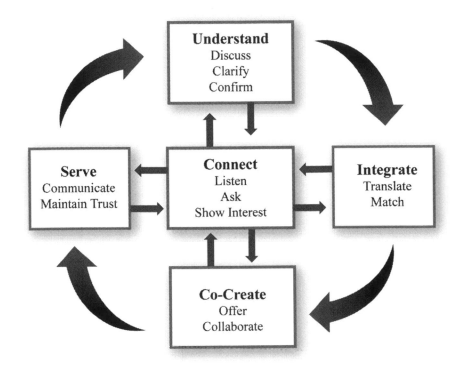

Unlike traditional sales, our model is not a linear equation. You don't conquer each step and then move on. This circular model emphasizes the continual focus on building and preserving the relationship. *(If you've read Coaching the Sale, or other materials related to coaching, you'll notice a similar approach. An equal partnership is also the foundation for productive coaching.)* We've already introduced the concept of connection. Now, let's explore how that initial connection extends into the whole client relationship.

Connect

Connect is the center of the partnering model. This is to remind everyone that you never leave that goal behind. Connecting, building and preserving the relationship are central components throughout the life of the business partnership. Connecting rejects the traditional competitive model. As we mentioned before, that model focuses on sales performance and the sales person. We're going to shift the focus to the client and building relationship with her. There are three fundamental elements to building relationship: *Listen, Ask* and *Show Interest.*

Listen

Listening might not appear to be anything special, but quality listening is a developed skill. In fact, there are five kinds of listening. We promised not to bog you down with unnecessary details, so we won't engage in an academic discussion of the various styles of listening. There are many other resources you can pursue for that. In fact, Tony teaches a workshop on connecting through Claymore Academy. Barbara coaches and presents custom workshops on all types of communication skills. For now, we'll train you on the one kind that is critical in connecting. We'll also caution you *against* a common listening style which actually disrupts connection. Let's start with that.

When a prospective client comes to you, you may focus on conducting a quality evaluation and providing outstanding professional advice. When you listen (with that focus in mind) you're thinking about analyzing data and presenting suitable solutions. You're listening to solve the problem or fix the need. This is called *evaluative listening*. In this listening mode, questions and responses are focused on evaluation and directed at giving sound advice. It leads the listener to ask for facts and data from the client. The focus is **not** on building a relationship bond. It's similar to going to a physician. Typically, the doctor asks diagnostic questions and then provides a solution to your concern. He does not do any of the following:

✓ Seek anything from you beyond diagnostic facts.

✓ Ask for your involvement in the solution *(except to tell you what to do)*.

✓ Build a personal bond.

The client is passive and disconnected when any professional employs this style of listening. The client just provides data and waits. Let's contrast that with connection-focused listening, which is called *empathic listening*. The empathic listener focuses solely on building relationship by demonstrating understanding to the speaker on all levels (facts and feelings). It lets the client know:

✓ I understand you!

✓ I value you!

✓ I am here for you!

When you're in this listening mode, the client does most of the talking. Your role is to affirm the client and build a sense of mutual appreciation and understanding. At this stage, the data you gather and your evaluation is far less important than communicating connection and understanding. For some, this may be a common listening style with clients. You do it naturally and spend a great deal of time focusing on building relationship. Those readers are well on their way to connecting with women investors. Others may be wondering: "How in the world do I do that?" It's very simple and incorporates the next two steps of *Ask* and *Show Interest*. But before we move on, let's emphasize the bottom line goal for listening as you connect. **The fundamental goal is to create a bond by listening well and communicating understanding.**

She Said/He Said:
What Women Want from Listening

Barbara:
The difference between the impact of *empathic* and *evaluative listening* is illustrated through a common experience in personal male/female relationships. In a typical scenario, a woman will vent about some issue. Her male companion will usually help by suggesting all sorts of solutions. She'll usually dismiss these and continue venting. The more advice he gives, the more upset/frustrated she becomes. Eventually, she bursts out with something like: *"Stop trying to fix me, I just wanted someone to listen and understand how I was feeling!"* My workshop audiences love this example. Every man (and woman) has had a similar experience! These situations are unfortunate. In most cases, men are really trying to help! Regrettably, the man uses *evaluative listening* when the woman really wants *empathic listening.*

Although the intention is good, the result is miserable! If this listening mismatch happens repeatedly, the relationship breaks down. Many broken relationships are caused by poor listening and communication skills. *Evaluative listening* (when used at the wrong time) can have a profoundly negative impact. In any interaction where preserving relationship is important, start with *empathic listening.* It's easy to switch to a solution focus as needed. It is much more difficult to re-connect if the wrong listening style has strained the relationship.

Tony:
Listening to connect is critical. Everyone can improve their listening skills. We all have stories of when we didn't listen well or we were not heard correctly. For the moment, I want to highlight another critical listening challenge–listening and communicating electronically! Electronic avenues are not good ways to connect and build relationship. In fact, they are dangerous. Email, text and other electronic pathways disburse data, but do not communicate feelings and intentions accurately. I recently had a painful reminder of this. I coach a sixth-grade girls' basketball team. I received an email from a player's mother informing me that her daughter had a sprained ankle and would miss an upcoming practice. Intending to lighten the mood, I shot back a teasing email writing: "She'll be fine, put some tape on it and get her to the game. There's no crying in basketball." Regrettably, the mother did not know my sense of humor and replied with a distressed email insisting that her daughter was too injured to practice. I immediately called to clear up the misunderstanding and apologize! Email, texting, words, inflection, facial expression and body language need to present a unified message for clear understanding. If any part of the communication is contradictory or missing, problems arise. We need to attend to our total communication picture in all its forms.

Ask

The goal in **Connect** is to listen empathically first. Then begin to ask questions that strengthen connection and seek her input. At this stage you are building bonds and showing you value her. You're also indicating immediately that she's an active member of the business partnership. While you're connecting and building relationship, you also gather financial information. It's a combined process. For those who are not used to listening empathically, while also gathering information, we wanted to provide some concrete examples. The following are samples of connecting questions that also gather financial information:

✓ What brought you to our meeting today?

✓ What's important for you?

✓ What are some interests or goals related to your finances?

✓ Who else in your life impacts your financial goals?

✓ Everyone has a different process for making decisions. How do you like to make important decisions?

✓ Some clients prefer to be very involved in the details, others prefer less involvement. What level of involvement might work for you?

✓ If you could reach all your financial interests, what would that look like?

✓ If you could meet only your minimal financial goals, what would that be?

✓ What kind of information or learning is important for you as we develop financial plans?

✓ My goal is to develop a great partnership. What's important to you as we work together?

Notice these broad, open-ended questions allow your female client to direct the conversation. They invite her involvement and interaction, which builds relationship. You also build relationship by listening empathically and validating what she is saying. *Validating* is a psychology term that sounds complex. In reality, it's a common place occurrence in our relationships. We validate anytime we commiserate with a friend. Think how many times you sit with buddies and exchange war stories of daily challenges. That is validating! To validate a client, acknowledge her comments and show understanding of her viewpoint. At the same time you're validating, listen for data that you can use later on when it's time to evaluate and offer guidance. Below are a few sample dialogues that illustrate exploring questions and validating responses to build relationship *and* elicit important data:

Sample Client Dialogue #1

New Client: "I've never been to an advisor before. I feel unsure of what I want. How can I plan, if I don't know what I want?"

Advisor: "Yes, there are a lot of choices and people often feel like they have competing interests. It can be a challenge to sort it out *(you validate her feelings and normalize her experience)*. I'm here to help you work through that. We'll work together to meet your interests and make sense of the options *(you show your support and your value)*. We can start by discussing your broad interests and make more detailed choices later on. Shall we start by exploring some general ideas of what's important for you related to your financial planning? *(You uncover what she wants.)*

Sample Client Dialogue #2

New Client: "I had a bad experience with an advisor before! You came highly recommended, so I thought I'd try again."

Advisor: "I'm sorry you had a bad experience *(notice that you avoid criticizing the other advisor, but still validate her experience)*. It's important to me that we have a good working relationship and I serve you well *(confirm yourself as a quality, concerned advisor)*. What's important for you as you we work together?" *(Engage her in telling you what matters to her. The other advisor may not have been bad; he may just have been ignorant of what she wanted in the relationship.)*

When you empathize, validate and ask client engaging questions you'll build relationship **and** gather a good deal of information. There is one more fundamental element to this process which leads us to our final step, *Show Interest.*

Show Interest

Show genuine interest in the client and her story! This sounds simple, but when you're thinking about getting to the next step, it can be hard to be truly engaged. The source for genuine interest comes from working through the **Call to Action** in chapters two and three: build strong motivation and shift to a connection focus. When you're eager to develop women clients and focused on connecting, an attitude of genuine interest will more naturally follow. This genuineness is vital! She will sense if you're less than authentic. A true desire to build a good professional relationship is more important than slick salesmanship. Remember, many women don't trust anyone who comes across like a traditional salesman. Women may interpret the traditional sales style as self-serving or uncaring. Equally dangerous is a connection style that is overly intimate. This may be misinterpreted as pursuit of her personally. Be very careful to approach women clients with a respectful professional demeanor, integrity and sincere interest. Up to 90% of communication is non-verbal. Your underlying attitude will come out! Those who focus on building professional relationship will reap the rewards of satisfied and loyal clients.

True Stories:
The Reward of Building Strong Relationships

We wrote this book during one of the most volatile markets of the past century (early 2009). During this period, we heard remarkable stories from advisors who had built strong relationships with customers. Clients offered emotional support **to the advisor,** expressing more concern for the advisor than their own financial portfolio! These advisors used varying financial tools. They did not have a magic product or process. Nor were they unusually brilliant in protecting clients from the financial downturn. The shared component of their success was a history of expressing genuine care for the client and acting accordingly. The clients felt confident that their advisor made recommendations based on true care and their personal financial downturn was not the advisors' fault. The client's trust in these advisors remained firm because of this established history of care. These strong relationships shielded advisors from a torrent of anger those with less loyal clients experienced. Not surprisingly, these advisors also report incredibly strong client retention, despite the panic. Building genuine relationship protects your business in good times and bad. Even better, it brings you great personal reward far beyond dollars!

In the rest of this book our **Live on the Street** entries are placed at the end of each chapter. Since this chapter is the longest, we thought there was value in providing several relevant examples. First, it reinforces the concepts to read peer experiences as they work with women. Second, it provides a needed change of pace for readers. The following **Live on the Street** entry is particularly notable. Patricia Bates is an outstanding professional who has worked up through the ranks to reach the executive level of Wells Fargo Advisors. She brings a valuable perspective as a leader and as a woman. Enjoy!

Live on the Street

Partnering with Women

We are fortunate to work with leaders in the financial services industry. Patricia Bates, a Regional President and Senior Managing Director with Wells Fargo Advisors, is a great leader who has rich experience in financial services. Patricia has spent her career in financial services and experienced many facets of the business, from advisor through local management up to executive leadership. She graciously gave us her time to share important lessons learned about partnering with women.

Tell us about what you have learned.

Before we get started I think there is an important warning I need to convey. There is no stereotypical male client or male advisor. Equally, there is no stereotypical female advisor or female client. It's important that anything I share be viewed as impressions, not absolute truths for everyone. I would never want to pigeon-hole advisors or clients. That would be a grave disservice to everyone!

What have you noticed about women clients over your career?

I notice that women clients often prefer to work with female advisors. Unfortunately, there are not enough female advisors in the industry, so it can be a challenge.

What do you think is the motivation for women to seek female advisors?

I think they would like someone who can relate. I tend to see it in two areas. First, women business owners have competing demands as they juggle their business and family responsibilities. They hope a female advisor will understand that reality. I also see women who become widowed or divorced look for a female advisor. They may not have a strong relationship with the male advisor who served the couple. In either case, I think the goal is to find someone that will understand them.

As a woman in a male dominated industry, what have you learned?

First, I've never thought of myself as a "woman" professional. I am a professional who happens to be a woman. That being said, I've brought a different perspective to the office. Sometimes, I see things from another angle and that viewpoint can add value. I've also tried to help male peers understand how their default style might impact interactions with me and other women.

What tips would you offer for greater success partnering with women clients?

1. **Be Patient.** A woman may not make a decision overnight. She may want to consult with others and mull a decision over.
2. **Design a Process for Connecting.** Be intentional when you meet with a woman client. Get to know her. Learn about her family, her likes, her dislikes, her goals and even her fears—*before* you present a product.
3. **Listen.** Refrain from interrupting. Keep listening!
4. **Be Inclusive.** Invite her to include any important people in meetings or decisions. She may want other people involved. If you invite involvement, you will learn what she wants.
5. **Be Professional.** Conduct and present yourself professionally. Your professional demeanor is important. Even though you may have conversation with women that includes personal information, don't mistake that for casual friendship.

We hope you enjoyed Patricia's input. Before we move on let's review briefly. Building a good connection is critical to partnering with women clients. You need to listen (a lot), ask open-ended questions and show genuine interest (in whatever the client wants to share). Your primary goal is to show care and compassion. We also want to thank you for your patience during our lengthy description of **Connect**. There is a reason for our wordiness. As you read on, you will notice that we return repeatedly to the connection skills of listen, ask and show interest. It's worth our joint effort to focus on these areas. They are critical to success. Now, let's move on.

Understand

The next stage in building a strong client relationship is the **Understand** phase. Reaching understanding is a process of discussing (giving and getting information) and then coming to mutual conclusions by clarifying and confirming. This is patently obvious. It does sound not much different from any standard practice of working with clients. However, it's important that advisors appreciate *the way* most women do this process. It's different than the common practice of many men.

Discuss: Giving Information to Women Clients

When making a decision, women tend to ask a lot of questions and seek more than one source of information. If a woman approaches you with a lot of questions, she is completing her due diligence in making a confident decision. If she wants more information (from you or others), it does not automatically mean she questions your expertise or distrusts you. She's probably making sure she gets all the facts. This style of gathering information is more time consuming than the average male style.

Such a protracted style of fact gathering may cause concern. Some advisors may fear women will consume all their time with endless questions. Just because she wants to gather lots of information does not mean you must meet all her fact gathering needs. You do not have to be the sole resource for everything she needs to know. You do need to facilitate her knowledge and help her get what she needs. Go back to the basic steps of connecting: *Listen, Ask* and *Show Interest.*

➢ *Listen.* For what she needs in order to move ahead.

➢ *Ask.* How you can facilitate her decisions.

➢ *Show Interest.* Validate her priorities in making a decision.

She'll likely work with you in keeping appropriate boundaries around your time investment. If you respectfully identify your limits and offer genuine assistance in getting answers, she'll probably honor your efforts and your time. However, your attitude is critical. If it appears that you're dismissing her or disinterested in helping her, you'll probably lose the client. If you help her connect to resources and support her need for information, you'll build relationship. In fact, women typically want multiple sources of information. You don't need to feel pressured to be her only source. Research shows that women value the experience and advice of other women. One powerful way to help her is to offer introductions to other satisfied women clients. This is a triple win:

1. It provides her a peer who understands and can support her process.

2. It allows you to delegate some of the decision-making dialogue.*

3. It also provides you a strong endorsement opportunity from a key a supporter.

* *Obviously, we encourage you to set appropriate expectations with a prospect about client comments on financial products and outcomes.*

Discuss: Getting Information from Women Clients

Women are generally more relationship focused and men are often more objective focused. As a result, women tend to make decisions in context of all their relationships. Their financial goals may be more focused on people, than on a list of objectives. They *may* come to you prepared with a list of goals. If so, plow ahead!

Then again, they may not have a prioritized list of goals. Very frequently women are the care-takers in the larger family unit. They may feel responsible for spouses, children, parents, siblings or in-laws. Their financial interests may be tied up with family relationships. If so, it is more difficult to identify a fixed list of priorities. It may look something like this:

"I want to care for my financial well being ... unless I need to care for a sick child ... except if I need to care for distressed siblings ... until I need to care for infirm parents."

This way of thinking does not lead to an easily definable list. There are too many moving parts and unknowns. Don't throw up your hands in frustration—yet! Return to the **Connect** skills: *Listen, Ask,* and *Show Interest*:

Listen. For the important themes and people that impact her financial goals.

Ask. Life-context questions that help you and her prioritize, such as:

✓ As you look at your whole life, what's important?

✓ As you make choices do you find yourself more focused on seizing opportunity or avoiding risk?

✓ How might that tendency inform your financial interests?

✓ We hope to reach all your financial goals. If events interrupt that, what are the most important things that must be in place for your financial confidence?

✓ Are there extended family members who have an impact on your financial goals and planning?

Contrast the previous questions with the objective list-focused questions below:

✓ What are your financial goals?
(Expects a pre-defined list.)

✓ What's your risk tolerance?
(Assumes she's defined it already.)

✓ What type of investing are you interested in?
(She may not know which products meet her interests.)

✓ I advise clients to invest in a balance of managed funds. Does that meet your goals?
(Little engagement for the client.)

There's nothing wrong with checklist-focused questions, if the client is prepared to discuss goals in that format. Some women may arrive with precisely such a list. However, we believe it is better to start with life-context style questions. If the client has a list, it will come out quickly. If she does not, the open style questions will engage her more quickly.

Show Interest. No matter how a client presents information and goals, showing interest is critical, even if she needs to talk story-style to reveal the final answer. Let her do it. This is how you continue to build relationship with her. Follow the story and interject with interested questions. You will be able to tease out the goals and information you need.

Clarify & Confirm

Also, during the **Understand** phase (and routinely in your communication) be sure to summarize and reflect back what you heard from the client. Summarizing and clarifying your understanding will benefit both of you. It will help her crystal-lize her goals in a concise form and you'll get the list you need. Clarifying will also assure that you're both on the same page. Never walk away from the conversation without completing this crucial step. If you're concluding a meeting during this phase, you may want to end by reiterating the next steps that you and she will take in the process. This provides her a sense of clear progress and shows the benefits of your service.

Integrate

Integrate is the logical next step. You probably do this without thinking and it may seem unnecessary to explain. However, we'll continue in order to fully explain the model. Also, we need to highlight how women have gotten lost at this stage. While in the **Understand** phase you were gather-ing what she wanted. Your role was facilitative. You actively listened and clarified her needs. In the **Integrate** phase your part in the partnership becomes more proactive. This is the stage when you offer options and help the client understand choices. It's important to explain financial products in meaningful language. If you've been savvy during the **Connect** and **Understand** phases you'll know if you can use financial jargon or whether you need to be more consumer friendly. During **Integrate**, you *Translate* and *Match:*

Translate

It's important to translate financial information into language she'll understand. This seems obvious, but apparently it's not common. In a recent survey, women were asked to pick adjec-tives that reflect their impression of financial services information. Here are the top four adjectives picked:

➢ Overwhelming

➢ Complicated

➢ Boring

➢ Foreign

Clearly something is not being translated! Nothing about financial information seems accessible, clear, helpful or understandable. We believe this is a holdover of the old attraction model which focused on making a good impression rather than partnering. When impressing the client is the focus, showing expertise is desirable. An expert can be obscure, complex and inaccessible. That's part of what makes the expert impressive! It raises the expert's status and lowers the client involvement. The expert has the authority and the skill; the client is a passive follower. This puts clients in a vertical relationship which reflects common male tendencies not overall female preferences. In contrast, our partnering model raises the client up on an equal footing with the advisor. It may also be true that the conversational disconnect is accidental. For professionals, technical terminology is their daily language. Experts may not realize how much lay people don't understand. It takes focused intention to communicate effectively.

In client relationships with women, it's important for her to have a functional understanding of products and services. If you listened well and asked insightful questions, you'll know some important things. You'll know how knowledgeable she is and how interested she is in the details. This will direct the particulars of your translation as you follow these principles:

1. Use language and terms she will understand.

2. Facilitate and support education as needed.

3. Make her feel comfortable. *(Use connection skills to gather, clarify and reflect back what she wants and needs.)*

Match

The matching process flows directly from translating. You're speaking a common language (that you both understand) and connecting her needs with your services. Matching is where your expertise takes over. In *Match* you step forward to offer the products and services that meet her needs. This is where you get to employ some *evaluative listening.* At this point, it's appropriate to focus on creating a good plan. Notice how far we are into the conversation before we've gotten to this point. For those readers who tend to be more direct, it may take a good amount of patience to wait this long before getting to action. Feel out the client as an individual, of course. Just remember, that if you jump to this stage too fast you risk frustrating women clients and damaging the relationship. That will not bring you the results you want. Also, remember the critical factor in *Match* is not the particular products you offer (of course, you will offer quality financial products). The key is *how* you partner with her to create a good plan, which brings us to the next stage, **Co-Create.**

Caution: *If there is a real mismatch between what you offer and what she wants, it's best to refer her to someone else immediately. We'll discuss the referral power of women more fully in a later chapter. Bottom line: women can be powerful promoters for your business. However, if they feel ill-served, their viral marketing will be toxic; they may forcefully warn their peers away from you. Alternatively, if you refer them wisely to someone else and communicate your service expertise, they are more likely to suggest peers who are well matched with your offerings.*

Co-Create

During **Co-Create** you suggest (with translation) the best options available and you work with her to create the best package for your overall business alliance. In **Co-Create** you *Offer* and *Collaborate*.

Offer

Generally, women prefer options and they do not like to be told what to buy. In addition, they want products/services to work for them and make sense in their lives. What's attractive to them depends on what's important for them. By the time you get to **Co-Create**, you should have a strong sense of how she wants to work with you around her money: high involvement or low involvement; high risk tolerance or low risk tolerance; security focus or growth focus; low fee/low service or high fee/high service. (If you don't, go back to **Connect & Understand**).

Offer continues the natural progression of translating and matching. You lead her to a range of choices. Suggest options and *directly connect these to how they meet her primary needs*. In addition, this may be an opportune time to outline your service guidelines with your offerings. Here and during *Collaborate* you can set service expectations with her. Women are usually cooperative. If they are reasonable and respectful, she'll probably respect your business parameters. If you present your service guidelines in a positive manner, focusing on what you do for clients more than what you don't do, there will be no reason for her not to cooperate. Then move to *Collaborate*.

Collaborate

Collaborate is nothing more than assuming that she is a full partner in the decision. The key is maintaining a collaborative attitude. This attitude is important. *Collaborate* is the opposite of the traditional sales approach which is directed by the sales person's agenda. In *Collaborate* there is an equal give-and-take. You're both working to find solutions, set goals and define success in your business relationship. If you've not done so before, now is the time to clarify what she can expect in terms of your time and service.

At this point you should have a well established connection and a good relationship foundation. If you've succeeded she'll hold you in high regard. She'll fully understand what you can *(and cannot)* provide. Setting goals and expectations collaboratively will go a long way to creating an easy business partnership. We're onto the final push for productive longevity: **Serve.**

Serve

The bottom line for **Serve** is to keep the relationship strong. In order to keep the relationship strong, you need to *Communicate* and *Maintain Trust.*

Communicate

We hear from many advisors that it's difficult to deal with client emotions around money. There is a temptation to ignore feelings when dealing with financial issues. We strongly encourage you to let feelings be a part of the communication, as she presents them. Ignoring the feelings will not make them go away. In fact, they'll probably increase with an added layer of frustration. This is a good time to use *empathic listening.* Relating and empathizing with the feelings expressed will strengthen the relationship and show that you're listening with genuine interest. It will reinforce your connection.

There's an added benefit to empathizing and letting emotions be expressed openly. It removes the burden from you to automatically fix something. Clients may just want to vent. They may not truly expect you to magically change a volatile market. If you allow them to vent, you'll have a better idea of the underlying source of the emotions. By the way, venting is not the same as blaming. Try to remember that venting frustration at a down market is not necessarily a judgment or attack on your service. It is important to maintain your objectivity and let the emotion dissipate like a steam release valve. Listen carefully. Then you can go about responding appropriately. Follow up and pursue any frustrations that are truly directed at your service.

Since you've partnered with the woman and co-created her financial plan, she'll have full ownership in the decisions. If she's upset with the result, you can gently review how she arrived at her decisions. Since you did not direct her, she will have little real foundation for blaming you for the outcome.

In **Co-Create** you established your working partnership expectations. Now when you communicate clearly (as you agreed) and openly work through emotions, you strengthen your connection and reinforce the relationship. The other key to **Serve** is *Maintain Trust*.

Maintain Trust

Maintaining trust is critically important in working with women. It's not complicated! Just don't promise anything you can't or won't deliver. If you slip-up accidentally, acknowledge the blunder immediately. There is great power in admitting culpability with women. In general, they do not see it as a sign of weakness. Rather, they'll view it as being honest and responsible. If you watch women, you'll notice they apologize easily and frequently. It's part of their focus on cooperative partnering and strong relationships. We believe the tendency for men to be competitive and their focus on presenting a strong image makes it more difficult for men to apologize. Apologizing may appear weak and lower status in a competitive environment. In contrast, a genuine and respectful apology will likely increase your status with women.

It shows that you value her and regard the relationship with her as important. The *Maintain Trust* equations are simple:

Say what you will do + Do what you say = Build trust

If you mess up + "Fess up"+ Repair = Preserve trust

In fact there is one vital warning that reinforces this concept: **Never break trust!** Most women are relationship focused; any hint of betraying trust can be a fatal blow to the partnership. Remember, women are generally cooperative, not competitive. If she feels that you're stepping over her to achieve a personal gain, you're on shaky ground. A move that makes her a loser and you a winner is a betrayal of the partner relationship. In contrast, men commonly accept and even expect competition in business partnerships. Striving to be top dog is normal and respected. Men may forgive predatory actions from a business partner out of respect for achievement and superior skill. This is not the general pattern with women. Preserving equality and cooperation is the common standard. Be careful to respect her interests in the partnership. Maintaining her trust is paramount!

This chapter is the longest in our volume. Thanks for hanging in with us! We felt it was important to present our partnership model comprehensively. Some readers may already be applying similar skills with current clients. Those readers can easily adapt established practices for a female client market. We encourage you to leap forward. There is great need and opportunity for skilled professionals. For those who desire to build new disciplines, we hope our model gives you a practical process for partnering effectively with women clients. Now, let's move on to the next level, reaching out to women for the opportunity to build connection.

Live on the Street

The Secret to Women Clients

It's been a tremendous joy to work with Craig Holmes an advisor with D.A. Davidson & Co., in Spokane, Washington. When Craig heard that I (Barbara) was working on this book, he volunteered to share his experience of working with women clients. Here is what he shared:

Tell me about working with women clients?

Once you know the secret, it's great!

Secret? What's the Secret?

The secret is listening to them about their lives, their families, their dreams, their concerns and even their fears **and** restraining yourself from talking until you've heard them out. Once you do that, you're all set. They become friends and loyal clients. From a man's perspective, it is showing respect. Listening to women is their currency of respect. Men show respect to each other in many ways, like a proper handshake. For women it's listening.

What's the impact on your business when you listen?

They bring me referrals. I'll give you an example. I have a female client with extended family. When we first met it became apparent that serious challenges were happening in the lives of her family members. The woman was clearly burdened by family issues. I put the paperwork away and said: "Today we are just going to talk. You're too distracted by these concerns to deal with business today". Then I listened to her and supported her. Eventually we did conduct our business, but I first cared for her as a person. Recently her adult daughters received a large inheritance. They handed over all their inheritance money for me to invest saying: "My mother says she trusts you."

That's a powerful story!

Yes! I don't have to prospect. Many clients refer me and people come to me! I'd also like to share another important thing, may I?

Yes, please!

When I first meet with couples, I always make sure that I address the wife directly and indirectly. I make sure that she understands and feels comfortable. Very often, when the husband asks a question, I will answer focusing more attention on making sure his wife is on board. If she's not comfortable with the situation, the deal will fall through. After they leave my office, the husband will listen to her concerns and they won't become clients. I've learned to always connect with the wife while I am attending to the husband's questions. Frankly, I don't want to work with couples unless they're both on board. I need the wife to be connected to what we are doing.

Why?

It will come back to bite me, if she doesn't completely trust me! I've discovered over the years that, if the wife trusts me, our relationship will be strong, even in rough markets. If there is any mistrust, then both parties tend to be upset during volatile markets. If the woman is on board, the communication is open, productive and trusting—even in the most difficult circumstances.

What else have you learned in working with women as clients?

Women are great clients financially! Once they're on board, they're very faithful and consistent. If they commit to an action they do it! They're much lower maintenance in that regard. However, you still need to attend to the relationship! You need to keep listening all along.

What's the break down of your client demographic?

I would say about 65% married couples, 25% single women and 10% single men

What would you say to advisors who are considering shifting their approach to connect more effectively with women?

I'd tell them to seek out women who can help them "see" through a woman's eyes. I have found professional women over the years that really helped me. I would not have been able to do it without helpful women who showed me how to work well with other women!

The Bottom Line

✓ Women need and are seeking financial-services partners. Women with financial advisors feel far more confident and knowledgeable than those without advisor support.

✓ We propose an equal partnership model as the foundation for working with women clients.

✓ The partnering with women is a circular process which includes: *Connect, Understand, Integrate, Co-Create* and *Serve.*

✓ Maintaining trust is a critical component in developing loyal women clients.

Individual Application

Use the space below to note facts and thoughts particularly relevant for you

Call to Action

1. **Review your client process.** Do you direct and advise your clients or do you collaborate equally in the decision making? Can you collaborate more? Identify how. Be specific.

2. **Evaluate your communication style.** How do you assess your client's financial fluency? Do you engage in "financial-speak" by using technical jargon? Create a list of common-language terms you can use to replace financial jargon.

3. **Consider your client service model.** How much do you collaborate with clients early in the relationship to set mutual expectations of the business partnership? Do you and the clients agree on what is expected from you? Revise as necessary.

4. **Attend to your emotional intelligence skills.** Do you empathize with client's feelings without falling into the trap of attempting to fix everything? How do you communicate, strengthen bonds and maintain trust to increase client loyalty? Improve where needed.

Personal Goals & Action Steps

Use the chart below to enter goals, action steps and target dates related to your goals

#1 → Goal	#2 Action Steps →	#3 Target Date

CHAPTER 5

Reaching Out To Her

Research shows that a disconnection exists between women investors and financial services. In this chapter we outline the facts about this female disengagement, draw conclusions about possible causes and propose a new path for reaching out to women clients.

Nuts and Bolts

Bridging the Gap

In the last chapter we touched on the gap between women and the financial services industry. Now let's get deeper into this issue. It's clear at this point, that women are economically viable. They are high earners and active buyers in the overall consumer marketplace. Now, let's consider their level of consumer activity in the financial world. Here's a sampling of this activity:

↑ Women open 89% of all new bank accounts.

↑ Women write 85% of all checks.

↑ Women make 80% of all financial decisions.

That's a lot of financial activity and that's just consumers. As we indicated earlier, women business owners also impact the marketplace. Let's recall these significant facts:

$ Women launch 70% of all businesses today.

$ Women own 10.6 million businesses.

$ Women owned businesses generate 2.6 trillion dollars in sales.

Considering this data, we should see a good productive relationship between women business owners and their financial providers. Unfortunately, this does not seem to be the case. Consider the following customer satisfaction data:

⬇ Two-thirds of women business owners find it difficult to work with their financial institutions.

⬇ One-third of women business owners feel discriminated against by their financial institutions.

Unfortunately, the banking world is not the only area that has left women wanting. Let's reiterate the sentiments of women about financial services information as a whole. Below are the top four adjectives women selected to describe financial services data:

☹ Overwhelming

☹ Complicated

☹ Boring

☹ Foreign

Clearly, financial services information is not perceived as helpful and accessible. Yet, we know that women recognize their financial needs and feel more confident with professional counsel. So we should see women looking to financial professionals for guidance. Sadly this is not the case! When asked where women would go for financial advice, financial professionals were **not** her first choice:

↓ Only 30% of women would seek out a financial advisor.

↓ Only 20% of women would go to a bank.

Compare that to other professional services. Do you think it's true that 70-80% of women don't go to a medical practitioner for medical help? How many women do auto maintenance themselves? Do they fix their own plumbing, wire their own houses, or install their own appliances? No! They get professional help in many areas of their lives. Yet, most women don't seek financial advice from financial professionals! Even though women are clearly active in the financial world and have obvious financial needs, they are not connected to the very industry designed to help them. Something is deeply wrong!

The financial industry has also done a lackluster job of attracting women professionals. Financial services lags far behind other fields when it comes to recruiting and developing women. In other businesses, women are fairly common:

↑ Half of all practicing attorneys are women.

↑ Nearly one-third of all practicing physicians are women.

↑ 46% of all management and professional positions are now held by women.

However, when we look at the financial services industry women are far more rare:

⬇ As few as 20% of financial planners are women.

⬇ Women make up only 16% of corporate officers in finance and insurance companies among the Fortune 500.

⬇ In brokerage firms, only 10% of brokers are women.

We believe holdovers from the past have kept women separated from the financial world as a whole. Some of these holdovers relate to the rapid professional and economic advance of women. Only recently have women engaged the marketplace enough to become financial professionals and clients. However, that does not explain the entire picture. Otherwise, women would have penetrated the financial world as much as other areas of business. Yet the disengagement is much more pronounced in this industry. Something is unique to the financial world. We believe old habits tied to past traditions are the culprit.

Traditions develop over time through the customs of a group. As an example, an afternoon of golf is a traditional networking event among business men. Yet, we know men who don't play golf and feel self-conscious when faced with the business golf outing. I (Barbara) have a client who leads a significant international organization. He is an avid biker but hates golf. It's been a challenge for him to work around the golf tradition without missing out on key relationship building opportunities. The financial world has its own traditions and culture. We believe this culture has hampered the increase of women financial professionals and clients. How? Well, one clue is a prominent icon. If you walk down Wall Street in New York City, you can't miss an impressive statue of this symbol. The bull! We believe the bull is symbolic of a tradition based on the attraction model. If you think about it, the traditional culture focuses on:

✓ Power. The bull icon that is a potent symbol of this focus.

✓ Status. The high lifestyle that is expected among financial professionals.

✓ Dominance. The gladiator-style competitiveness that is encouraged.

✓ Expertness. The jargon that is the commonplace.

To be fair, there is absolutely nothing wrong with strong competitive dominance! We are not advocating a world without healthy competition. However, we are focusing on what appeals to female clients. There is very little in the Wall Street culture that appeals to the female sense of connection and cooperative partnering.

She Said/He Said:
Missed Opportunities Using Old Tactics

Barbara:
While researching the failure of traditional marketing to reach women investors I had a personal revelation. That's it! No wonder I don't go running to financial services on my free time. The presentations I've attended focused on expertness and delivered a massive data dump of jargon. In addition, the visual impression focused on high style. Everything conveyed the image of expertness and elitism. That was done very well! Unfortunately it did not entice me to engage. Financial jargon is not a dialect I speak fluently (although I am more fluent than many because of my financial clients). Also, very little was done to connect with my interests. The elitism, though stunning, was not necessarily endearing. This might surprise you, but extravagant displays of status can sometimes backfire.

Is the advisor interested in *helping* clients or *using* clients to get rich? Don't get me wrong, I appreciate luxury and I am no socialist! I think the opportunity to build wealth is tremendously important for individuals, communities and nations. I am happy for people to earn high reward, but not at the expense of others. Perhaps, it is my female viewpoint. I want an advisor to work for me and with me, rather than use me as a tool in his wealth acquisition competition. Please don't presume that my experience reflects those of every woman. I can only speak for myself. However, discovering that many other women feel the same has been wonderfully validating! If you want to find out what women clients in your community want – go ask them! I am sure it will be a productive and profitable experience!

Tony:

Recently, I spoke to an advisor who had an opportunity to address fifty female prospects at one time. He was invited to address this group of women business leaders and was not sure what to say. I asked him what he thought he would say. "I plan to tell them about my dynamic portfolio rebalancing process, then give a market overview." I politely said, "Who cares?" Instead, I urged him rather to present a few points about the power of the female investor, the trends that we write about in this book. I also asked him to engage the audience about why a woman should embrace a financial plan and what value a qualified professional might offer to help her manage it. Furthermore, I asked him to equate the importance of a female's commitment to a professional-aided plan to her desire to consult with her medical doctors on a regular basis. He responded favorably, saying: "You know, each time I have explained my dynamic portfolio rebalancing process to a female prospect, I have never won the business." I shot back the old adage: "People don't care what you know, until they know that you care." It seemed to work for him. Words matter! Words can help create a positive connection, actions go even further! Create the experience you desire for your clients and prospects, even more so for your females clients and prospects.

The traditional financial marketing also doesn't connect to what's important to women when buying a product or service. Market research shows that women are *contextual* shoppers. They look for how the product or service makes sense within their lives. Recently, Ace Hardware discovered the power of using contextual marketing to women. Through internal research, Ace discovered they were missing a huge customer base in their traditional stores. The data showed that women were 50% of their shoppers and influenced 80% of the buying decisions. Perhaps this came as a surprise, since hardware is not usually considered a feminine product. As a result, headquarters initiated a female-focused marketing campaign and created a new store design. The new store layout included consumer-friendly signage and display vignettes showing the product in a household setting. In addition, the shelves were streamlined to make selection easier. When a full store model of the new design was unveiled to 1,200 True Value franchise operators, 60% leaped to adopt the new layout.

The sporting goods industry has also discovered the value of reaching out to women. Brooks Running Company found that women think differently about how sports fit into their lives. If you ask a woman what "sport" she played last week, she may have no response. If you ask a woman what "fitness or workout" she did last week, she'll have a ready answer. Women use exercise equipment to stay fit and keep healthy. They don't view it as a "sport". When the Brooks Running Company began branding around *fitness* rather than *sports* they saw a significant change. Footwear sales rose 20% in 2007 and women's sales were equal to men's for the first time. Women now make up 57% of all running shoe sales and 70% of all running apparel. Jim Monahan, VP of footwear at Asics America, explains it well: "Women of all ages are driving the business and because of that trend we have focused and expanded our selections across the board." These companies are now successfully reaching the female market by adapting their messages specifically for women. What they were doing before just didn't connect with the way women operate. Without the effort to think differently and change the approach they might've written women off as low value customers, not worth it! Instead, they found out how to connect and are reaping the benefits of increased sales and a whole new customer base.

Sony also created a win by researching women's interests and built stores specifically to meet these priorities. You will find Sony Style store to be:

> ➤ **Appealing.** They designed elegant displays with a concierge desk.

> ➤ **Contextual.** They presented electronics in living-room settings.

> ➤ **Comfortable.** They built-in wide aisles to accommodate families and strollers.

> ➤ **Accessible.** They included signs to translate jargon into common language.

> ➤ **Convenient.** They stocked a focused selection of products that were light, easy to use and mobile.

The end result was a hit for both women *and* men. As David Syracuse, Senior VP for Sony retail stores says: "We found that men wanted the same things--both sexes wanted gadgets to be light, easy to use and mobile."

Unfortunately, some mistake marketing to women as "pinking" up the products and services. This approach is unappealing on multiple levels. First, extreme feminizing turns off male clients. Equally damaging, bungled feminizing attempts backfire with women too! Take for example Seduction wine. A bottle of Seduction is encased in a red gauze sheath, like sexy lingerie. The label suggests a heated romance plot: "voluptuous, with sensual flavors and a velvet kiss." Mary Ewing-Mulligan, President of the International Wine Center in New York City and author of several books on wine, sums up her frustration with clumsy feminine marketing like this: "I wish they wouldn't resort to stereotyping and patronizing us." Mary's comments reflect the overall consumer research on botched feminizing. Women are turned off when marketing and sales methods appear condescending. So take heart, you don't have to turn everything pink in order to market to women. Smart marketing to women is going to appeal to women and is not going to turn off your male clients! In fact, men will likely value an approach that offers more appeal, comfort, accessibility and convenience.

What to Do

Fortunately, we don't need to reinvent the wheel to improve for women. The first key is to pay attention to what market research experts have already discovered. Start with the same concepts: appealing, comfortable, convenient, accessible and contextual. Let's consider what this might mean for advisors and for female clients. For our purposes we will group them into two frameworks that can act as a foundation for your approach. The first is focused on engaging the client in ways that are appealing, comfortable and convenient. The second is focused on being understandable to the client by being contextual and accessible. We call the two frameworks *Create a Welcome* and *Be Relevant.*

Create a Welcome

What does appealing, comfortable and convenient mean to women clients? First, let's remember what it is not. It's not like the traditional methods. We believe the traditional methods were based on an attraction model instead of a connection model. Under an attraction model, the focus is on showing superiority and elitism. This can be very impressive, but not necessarily effective. Since women generally prefer a connection focus, creating a warm welcome is more likely to be successful. When you think of a warm welcome what does it feel like? A warm welcome makes you feel comfortable and at ease. You feel valued and your host thoughtfully anticipates your desires to help you feel at home. *You feel invited to, relax, participate and engage. You do not feel intimidated or inferior.* A warm welcome is also pleasantly appealing. You want to come in and enjoy the setting that was thoughtfully prepared for you. You can create a warm welcome in any environment, formal or informal. Do not confuse a warm welcome with automatic casualness or informality. Whether it is a formal event or a casual gathering, make sure your efforts are attractive *and* increase client comfort with you and the topic. Orient participants so that they feel at home. Guests should feel included and valued. The particulars of this will depend on your community and your client niche. What feels welcoming in one community may not work in others. We would not presume to make specific recommendations. You know your culture better than anyone. Here's the bottom line: when you're developing materials and planning events think about how to create an inviting, engaging, comfortable and appealing setting.

Be Relevant

Contextual is a fancy name for making sure something is adapted to make sense within an individual's personal context. In effect, the person will be able to "get it". I (Barbara) once heard a radio interview with Dr. Michael Roizen, a physician and bestselling author on living well. In the interview he recalled how years ago he could not get patients to change their bad habits. These habits were very dangerous, but no matter how many times he urged patients to eat well, stop smoking and begin exercising they would not do it. The patients were told repeatedly about damage to their hearts, lungs, and arteries, but to no avail. Then Dr. Roizen told a patient that unhealthy habits had created a body much older than the patient's real age. The patient sat up and took notice! Dr. Roizen's book *RealAge: Are You as Young as You Can Be?* was based on this premise. It was a smash hit! It became a New York Times bestseller and was translated into more than 20 languages. When patients realized what they were doing was adding 5, 10, even 15 years to their actual age, they "got it". Who wants to have the body of a 55-year-old at age 40? Nobody! Dr. Roizen contextualized his message. You can do the same. Make sure your messages to clients communicate what "it" will mean in daily living, now and in the future. The more you make it relevant, the more impact it will have.

Reaching out to her is just another way of connecting with her. When you fix your focus on making her feel valued, engaged and included, your specific methods will unfold naturally. If you find yourself struggling to apply the concepts in your practice, we invite you to include women professionals as part of your counsel. They will guide you in the right direction. Ultimately, you can't go wrong by focusing on being relevant, engaging and welcoming.

Live on the Street

Reaching Women

Michelle Alberda has worked in the financial planning industry for nine years. Currently, she is a certified financial planner (CFP) with a Fortune 500 financial planning company. Michelle is also the co-author of "SKIRTworking: How to Network Using SKIRT" (Sharing Knowledge Information and Resources Together). SKIRTworking teaches women professionals how to develop a thriving referral based business using relationship networking. Michelle and her SKIRTworking co-authors: Stacey Fleece and Michelle Balog created SKIRTworking after the dramatic success of their networking alliance. Michelle generously shared her marketing insights.

The past 18 months (2008/2009) have been really stressful in the financial services industry. How are you doing?

Well, I am glad you asked. Before I share tips on marketing to women it's important for people to know if it works. I had my best year ever in 2008 and this year (2009) looks to be even better. I believe the same is true for my co-authors, Michelle Balog and Stacey Fleece. All three of us are in seriously stressed industries: financial services, real estate and mortgage banking. If we're having our best years now, it works!

Your focus is helping people market effectively. Tell us about marketing to women.

> ➤ Think about your conversational style! For goodness sake, please don't trot out those sports analogies that men use all the time. I can't tell you how many men (who want me as a client) use sports as a primary relating tool. I don't care about sports! Even more, the sports analogies don't make sense to me. I don't think they realize how much they do it. Equally bad is using stereotypical feminine analogies. I personally find shopping analogies so trite, I'm offended. As if I am only interested in shopping!

➤ **Don't be patronizing!** Many clients come to me, because they've been patronized by male advisors. Here's an example: One client inherited a large amount of money from her father. Her father's advisor was a family friend. Even though she is an intelligent adult, the man became "parental" around her. He told her what to do every time they met. She couldn't wait to leave him!

That is a great warning of what <u>not</u> to do. What advice do you have about what <u>to do</u>?

➤ **Use universal anecdotes & analogies.** Create talking connections that are familiar to everyone. There are lots of ordinary subjects that make good anecdotes and analogies. Stay away from stereotypical subjects for either gender.

➤ **Get around women!** Join a women's professional or community association. Many groups have open membership. I belonged to a women's professional organization and there was only one male member. He got a lot of attention! Be sure to participate regularly and contribute, being a token member will not cut it. If that feels too uncomfortable, then get around more women anyway you can. It will help you understand women better. It will also help you connect to women clients and their referral network.

Do you have ideas on marketing events?

I have a well-established referral network with complementary professionals. Instead of inviting my clients to a dinner event, I called my referral source and asked her to bring her clients. I treated them all to dinner. We got to know each other and I started to build relationships with new people.

Are there other helpful tips you would like to share?

Yes! I learned to have the right balance of respectfully guiding without dominating. Women don't want to be told what to do. However, they do want to be educated and given options. I have men and women clients, as well as couples. I make sure that everyone is treated respectfully. As result, I have great client retention and annually receive superior client satisfaction scores on client surveys.

What are examples of respectful guidance?

1. **Speak English!** I try to use common language as much as possible and avoid industry jargon. I can't expect lay people to understand financial jargon. Both male and female clients appreciate this.

2. **Expect to Review & Re-educate.** Financial products are my business but they're not a daily topic for most clients. I can't expect them to remember all the nuances of complicated financial instruments. I revisit and review repeatedly, asking them to stop me, if they're already fully versed on the details. Clients appreciate the review and are free to stop me, if they don't need the reminder.

3. **Be a Proactive Guide.** Be proactive. For example, I meet with my clients every six months faithfully. They know when we're meeting again and the purpose for our next visit. I also actively facilitate their best interests related to financial planning. For example, I encourage them to do an estate plan. If this falls through the cracks continually, I let them know that I will invite an attorney to our next meeting to help them get started. I advocate for their best interests and help them be accountable. They appreciate it.

How do you build trust with clients?

➤ **Be Transparent!** I am very open, direct and honest about my business practices. I tell clients in the first meeting:

1. How I make money as a financial planner.
2. How the fee structure works.
3. How the company works.
4. How I make product recommendations and why.
5. Where they can save fees and where it is not worth it (and why).

➤ **No Surprises!** The goal of being transparent is to set an honest and open working relationship with no surprises. I never want my clients to feel cheated, deceived or that I have ulterior motives. If they know how everything works upfront, they're not going to be wondering why I suggested this or that. I've always been transparent, but in today's environment, people are very suspicious. It benefits everyone to be upfront!

➤ **Focus on the client, not self-promotion.** The clients care about what you can do for them, not your great success. Focus your attention on them, not yourself.

The Bottom Line

✓ Women are disconnected from the financial services industry. Up to 80% of women **do not** go to financial professionals for guidance.

✓ Traditional financial marketing doesn't match women's interests or preferences.

✓ Exaggerated feminizing attempts backfire for all customers.

✓ Connecting with women well will significantly increases sales.

✓ Companies that have marketed specifically for women have increased success with both female and male customers.

Individual Application

Use the space below to note facts and thoughts particularly relevant for you

Call to Action

1. **Review your materials.** How many of them have these qualities?
   o   Overwhelming
   o   Complicated
   o   Boring
   o   Foreign
   Decide what needs to change to increase accessibility.

2. **Examine client events**
   o   Are events attraction focused?
       ▪   Design a connection-focused approach.

   o   Are clients passive listeners?
       ▪   List specific methods to engage client participation.

3. **Increase contextualization.** Does your approach expect the client to understand financial jargon? Translate jargon and connect financial products/services to everyday client experience.

Personal Goals & Action Steps

Use the chart below to enter goals, action steps and target dates related to your goals

#1 Goal	→	#2 Action Steps	→	#3 Target Date

CHAPTER 6

Expanding Connection Exponentially

Continuing to build a client network is a never-ending job for financial advisors. Women can be powerful advocates who freely and vigorously promote you. Once you have established your skill in connecting and partnering with women clients you can activate the power of the female marketing network. We tell you how!

Nuts and Bolts

Viral Marketing: Woman Style

For financial services professionals, expanding the client list is a never-ending goal. Even those advisors with a large and profitable client base must replenish with new clients over time. Ideally, clients seek you! That's the intent of viral marketing. The internet site Wikipedia describes viral marketing as:

> "Viral marketing and viral advertising refer to marketing techniques that use pre-existing social networks to produce increases in brand awareness or to achieve other marketing objectives (such as product sales) through self-replicating viral processes, analogous to the spread of pathological and computer viruses. It can be word-of-mouth delivered or enhanced by the network effects

of the Internet. Viral marketing is a marketing phenomenon that facilitates and encourages people to pass along a marketing message voluntarily." (www.wikipedia.com)

If you continue reading the Wikipedia entry, you'll find many examples related to technology: internet, blogs, video clips etc… The hook in most viral marketing is publicity stunts in the name of product promotion. This can be a very effective style of marketing, but it is based on the attraction model. Some surprise stunt attracts you and spurs communication. When seeking to interest female clients, it's important to remember what women find appealing, connection instead of attraction. Therefore, we will move away from the publicity-based approach and focus on spurring female viral marketing by expanding connection.

Women have a connection focus when seeking products and services. They use relationship rather than publicity stunts or advertising as their resource. Consider the following current market research:

- ✓ Women use family and friends to find product/service information. All other marketing formats (print, TV, and internet) lag far behind personal connections.

- ✓ In a recent retail purchasing study of affluent women (income over $308,000), 96% of women learned of brands from personal relationships.

- ✓ One-third of women do not trust sales people to give them accurate information.

This last statistic reveals an intriguing trend. Since women value relationship, a sales person relating to the customer should be an effective method, as opposed to impersonal avenues like the internet or other media. However, a full third of women presume **all** sales people are untrustworthy. We believe that a history of *selling* instead of *serving* the customer may have soured women's trust in the sales relationship. Trust is a big factor for female consumers. Trust influences not only sales relationships but also product choices. Consider how much trust influences women's purchases:

- ✓ 70% are willing to pay more for a brand they trust.

- ✓ 72% say a trusted brand makes their life easier.

- ✓ 83% will recommend a brand they trust.

Women want every part of the purchasing process to be trustworthy. It avoids hassle. Much of the market research indicates that women today feel very pressed for time. They don't want to waste time or money. Untrustworthy products or services mean they have to spend more time and more money to get the job done.

Women want reliability whether they're seeking a product, service or even a referral. That's why women use their personal relationships as referral sources. They're confident a friend or family member will offer honest and trustworthy advice. It makes sense that these trustworthy relationships are the primary conduit for information. This referral network is a two-way street. Women ask advice from other women and they also actively promote preferred services to their peers. This has bottom-line impact for you. Consider this:

- ✓ Women are people loyal, not institution loyal. They will stay (or move) with the professional rather than with the institution.

- ✓ Women directly refer two times more than men.

- ✓ Women will recommend a trusted product/service three times more frequently than men.

This is fabulous news for financial professionals. If you can connect and develop a trustworthy relationship with women clients, they will likely:

➢ Stay with you. **Her value to you = 1 x (years in your career).**

➢ Make many referrals. **Her value to you = 2 x (all your male client referrals).**

➢ Recommend you even more. **Her value to you = 3 x (all recommendations from male clients).**

She Said/He Said: Women:
A Viral Marketing Bonanza

Barbara:
I never thought much about the female referral network until I researched this book. The more market data I read, the more it confirmed my life experience. Women have been my primary network for consumer information. If you eavesdrop on women, you'll hear lively discussions about best sources for desired products and services. In fact, this network of women is so well trusted that even strangers will spontaneously engage in *woman to woman* marketing. It's often initiated when a woman notices an accessory or item of clothing and compliments the other woman spontaneously. Immediately, the conversation turns to best places to shop for similar items. This happens everywhere: in the workplace, on the street corner, at the store counter or even out on the town!

Women actively promote products and services between each other. It's a white hot network! I live in a newer neighborhood where all the homes were built with unfinished basements. Soon, homeowners began finishing their lower levels. Somebody in the neighborhood found *Basement Bob*. He was everything a woman looks for in a service provider: reasonably priced, trustworthy and capable. If you were interested in finishing your basement, all you had to do was ask a woman neighbor: "How do I get a hold of *Basement Bob?*" and the network would start up.

The most recent *Bob* customer would pass along the phone number and *Bob* got a new job. Here's the amazing thing, *Bob* **never** advertised. Even more amazing, most people didn't know *Bob's* last name or the name of his business. Yet, he had jobs scheduled over a year in advance. *Basement Bob* became the preferred basement finisher for the entire neighborhood **without doing one thing to market himself!** He provided good service at a reasonable cost and the women promoted him voluntarily and vigorously. Wow. Now that's what I call expanding connection exponentially!

Tony:
In my life, I have a similar story but it is through family connections rather than neighbor networking. My brother's wife discovered *Handyman Paul*. He did a good job, was reasonable and reliable. Soon *Handyman Paul* was recommended to my wife. He did a good job for us and my wife recommended *Handyman Paul* to her mother. Then *Paul* got work from another sister-in-law and family friends as well. His name and good reputation have been spread by all the women in my family and their friends. I personally know of over a quarter of million dollars in income earned by *Paul* from just a few families. This for a handyman! Similar to *Basement Bob, Paul* did not spend one dime on marketing or advertising to receive these jobs. They were handed to him by the recommendations of women based on his quality work. We'd all like to have the time and money we spend on marketing available for other purposes. What a dream: do quality work and the customers flood in on their own!

Inspiring Female Viral Marketing

You want such a great network and we want to help you. First, we must emphasize that the female viral marketing network is already active and flowing. You don't have to make it from scratch or get it moving. It's there and running hot all the time. The key for financial professionals is to become accepted into the network and be positively promoted within it.

It's equally important that you don't inadvertently join the negative network that runs alongside the promotion channel.

When women network about products and services they frequently give *all* their feedback into the *woman to woman* viral network. They don't just promote the positive providers, they also actively warn their peers against poor service. If two women are talking about local handymen, the woman who's had experience with local carpenters may offer the something like the following example:

> *Positive Promotion:* "Definitely call Joe at Ace Handyman. He was timely, reasonable and did a good job. I would highly recommend him. I will get you his number." (*Actively promotes by following up later with contact information.*)

> *Neutral Offer:* "I heard Mary say good things about Bob at Bob's Fix-it, so you might want to call Mary and see what she has to say. (*Offers alternatives, but, is less likely to be as proactive with neutral suggestions.*)

> *Negative Warning:* "Stay away from Harry at Household Houdini, he was a disaster! He screwed up the job, made a mess and wouldn't fix his mistakes. Make sure you don't get him!" (*As active with warnings as promotions, she may repeat the warning about the bad referrals when she follows up about her positive promotions.*)

If another woman is present, the second woman will jump in with her own recommendations. If the women concur, then the force of the advice is magnified. The positive advertising is now strongly positive, likewise the negative advertising is also reinforced. The power of both increases exponentially! The more a woman passes along toxic advertising, the more negative power it gains. Likewise as positive referrals increase, the force of the promotion is strengthened. Women go to several sources and overlapping networks. You absolutely want to be the advisor that comes up positively in multiple circles. Equally important, you do not want to be the advisor affiliated with repeated toxic advertising. The ultimate goal is to be a preferred advisor in multiple, overlapping female networks.

The first step in becoming a preferred advisor in female viral marketing networks is to remember the cardinal rule of working with women. It's all about the relationship. Just like the **Connect** phase you:

Listen

Ask

Show Interest (be genuine)

For the viral marketing process we will switch the order to: *Listen, Show Interest and Ask.* You might be wondering why we keep repeating the same principles of *Listen, Show Interest* and *Ask* in different contexts. Please don't be bored or offended. We keep using these principles for two important reasons. First, they are the foundation of building good relationships with women, no matter how you are working with them. Second, you don't have to reinvent the wheel at every turn. If you become accomplished at some essential skills, you can apply them successfully in many different situations without having to adopt multiple new methods.

Listen

Women promote those who have served them well and they do it spontaneously. The first step is to listen for service needs while you work with her. Listen and then serve her well. Also, listen for clues related to friends and family. Clues will probably come out in stories she tells. The wise advisor will not tune-out during story time. Instead he'll pay close attention to the people mentioned and the needs the advisor can fulfill. This leads to the next steps of *Show Interest* and *Ask*.

Show Interest

Women are focused on trust in any relationship including professional service relationships. Showing genuine interest (and action) in helping her builds trust. If you build trust, she will promote you. This is how *Basement Bob* and *Handyman Paul* got years of work without any active marketing. That may be enough. However, you can reach the next level by being invited into the network. You do that by asking questions and aligning yourself strategically with her network's interests.

Ask

The foundation of any invitation into her viral marketing network is a strong trust relationship. For that you excel at **Connect, Understand, Integrate, Co-Create** and **Serve**. Once you have achieved high trust you are prepared to move forward. However, if you don't have confirmation of full satisfaction, verify that first. It will be a double negative if she's not fully satisfied and she thinks you're using her to get to her friends.

Once you've confirmed a strong bond you can seek direct entry into her network. Wonderfully, you provide a necessary life service. Financial planning is not like the purchase of an appliance, only an occasional need. She regularly needs a financial advisor and so does everyone she knows. You can reach her network by offering to meet their needs. Strategic questioning will provide important information. Below are examples of interest-gathering questions. Notice that we start by checking service satisfaction and soliciting honest feedback.

> *"My industry has not always met the needs of women well. Am I meeting your interests well?"*

> *"What has been most helpful for you as we've worked together?"*

> *"I want to make sure that I serve you and others well. What kinds of concerns do you hear when you talk with women friends?"*

"Financial services and products can be very complex. How do you think I could help make this topic more accessible for your friends and others?"

"What kind of outreach effort might be helpful to your friends and other women you know?"

"People are so busy these days. I sure don't want to be an annoyance. As you talk with friends what is the preferred way to for someone like me connect and be a help?"

These questions have the side benefit of eliciting important information about your service to her. If you're not already actively seeking her feedback, these will help you do it. As you ask these questions, be sure to listen for (verbal and non-verbal) cues about her receptivity. If she appears hesitant, in any way, quietly back off. Your goal is to prompt an eager advocate. Hesitancy indicates that she is not really your advocate or that she's uncomfortable with inviting you into her network. When you feel resistance, we recommend you back off and then return to the connection phase to build a higher level of trust.

In some cases a woman may be a strong advocate, but not wish to invite you into her network with a direct introduction. She may wish to refer by giving friends your name, rather than invite you to a meeting or facilitate a personal connection. If that's her preference – go with it. You'll not win any friends by pushing for a personal introduction to her peers. If she feels pressed, she may acquiesce to you and then apologize to her friends for the intrusion, rather than say "No" to you. In that case, you'll present yourself to a group of women who'll listen politely but may secretly resent you for the coerced meeting.

If this seems complicated and fraught with potential land mines, don't be overly concerned. The fundamental skills of *Listen* and *Ask* will serve you well. She will communicate (either verbally or non-verbally) her level of willingness. It's just a matter of tuning in, listening and showing genuine interest in helping her and her friends. She will guide you, if you take the time to listen. Remember if you serve her well, she will:

1. Be a loyal customer.

2. Refer you twice as often as male clients.

3. Recommend you three times as often as male clients.

You can receive all that even without being invited into her network. Imagine what you can do if she invites you in!

In Conclusion

Thank you for joining on this journey into the world of women clients. Like any good guides, we sifted through a mountain of information and important data to bring you the most pertinent facts. We synthesized complex ideas into simple operating framework. We outlined important skills for your application. We stuck to core principles to give you the freedom to create a personalized plan. We put together a guidebook that we hope is streamlined enough to be manageable and detailed enough to be meaningful. Finally, it is our hope that we:

➢   Provided relevant data

➢   Helped you navigate the topic

➢   Prepared you to succeed

➢   Offered you insider tips

➢   Gave you effective tools

➢   Inspired you to action

It is now up to you! You have full freedom to take this as far as you can go. We invite and encourage you to fill the need. There is vast potential and it is ever increasing. Our final thoughts are summed up best by a famous quote:

"Luck is what happens when preparation meets opportunity."

The author, Lucius Annaeus Seneca, is probably less familiar than the quote. Seneca was a philosopher who lived around the turn of the century, the *first* century. Seneca authored this famous statement nearly 2000 years ago. Luck has always come to those who prepare and go for it. It was true 2000 years ago and it's true now. There is no new magic, nothing more, nothing better, nothing to wait for. The opportunity is there, take up your preparation. Luck is waiting!

Now we invite you to enjoy our last **Live on Street** interview with Beth Rosenwald. Beth has 20 years of experience in financial services and gave us powerful insight into a changing industry. We are heartily grateful for the valuable experience she, and all our contributors, offered for our benefit. Turn the page, it's worth it! Then keep reading and you will find your last **Bottom Line, Individual Application, Call to Action** and **Personal Goals & Actions Steps**. Finally, if you are interested in learning more about us, turn to the end of the book. There is more there, as well. Thank for spending your time with us. Our lives are dedicated and committed to outstanding service to clients (both our clients and your clients). It is our goal to work with you to build extraordinary success with profound significance.

Live on the Street

Expanding Your Network

Beth Rosenwald is Senior Vice President and Branch Director of RBC Wealth Management in Baltimore, Maryland. She has 20 years of experience in financial service. We were thrilled to have her input. Beth talked with us and shared how much the industry has changed in relationship to women and all clients. She has a very clear picture of how to expand your network in the current environment.

Tell us about marketing to women clients

The industry is coming around related to women clients. Fifteen years ago when they tried to market to women, they wrapped a pink bow around old methods and thought they were marketing to women. Of course, it didn't work.

What does work with women?

Well, it depends on the market and the mood of clients in general. In the rocking '90s I conducted large, fun events for women that included fashion, food and finance. We ran these events twice a year for at least three years running. They were very successful. They got bigger and more fun. In the current market, we've focused on small intimate events with professionals who can educate women on life concerns. I work with an attorney and a physician. We do a Health, Wealth and Family event. These are much smaller, a maximum of thirty participants. When you are addressing life concerns you have to have a small audience, so people feel comfortable asking questions. I target women, but I also pay attention to the market and the country's overall mood.

You've been in this industry a long time. What changes have you seen?

I've seen many changes. The old style marketing and sales tactics never worked for women and now they don't work for men either.

Can you give us an example?

When I started people did cold calling. You could attract clients by offering attractive options on the phone. That just does not work at all anymore. There was also a pretty clear equation on results. If you made so many calls, you could expect to end up with a certain percentage of prospects and then land a group of clients from those prospects. The old equations don't fit now. The numbers game is obsolete.

What does work?

Well, the good news is that what works for women, is what is needed for everyone now. You need to invest in a community with a long-term focus on developing deep roots and connections. It's a much deeper and longer sales cycle.

What does that look like?

> You need to focus on building relationship with all potential clients.
> You need professional depth and breadth. A focus on transactional hits isn't sustainable.
> You need a clear identity in terms of:
>> o Brand
>> o Services
>> o Products
>> o Market
> Just like you have short, mid-term and long-term investing strategies. You need the same with your marketing and business strategies.

How has that changed advisors?

You see many more teams now. It's really tough to be a solo advisor. You need peers with different strengths to bring broader and deeper services. You need to build relationships with teams and with clients.

What's important to clients?

For women it's totally about trust. They need to know you. If they like you, then they trust you. If they trust you, then they will invest with you. Currently, every client is focused on trust. People are cynical, scared and suspicious. Building trust is important now for all clients.

What else is true for clients?

Clients are much more educated now. The internet has changed our world. People have a lot more access to information. They ask questions. They want to be educated. We all have to up our game in educating and working cooperatively with clients. This is not just an issue for women. The skills that are needed for women clients are now needed for all clients.

The Bottom Line

✓ Women transmit marketing information through personal relationships in a woman-to-woman marketing conversation.

✓ Women will actively advertise both negatively and positively by providing all their feedback while engaging in female viral marketing.

✓ Advisors can be positively promoted just by becoming a trusted advisor.

✓ Advisors can be further promoted when invited into a woman's network.

✓ Following the woman's cue is critical to positive promotion.

✓ Quality connection skills—*Listen, Show Interest* and *Ask*—will guide the advisor to increase connection exponentially with women clients.

Individual Application

Use the space below to note facts and thoughts particularly relevant for you

Call to Action

1. **Assess referral sources.** How many referrals come from personal connections? This is a good measure of how trusted you are by all your clients. For women it is critical, if you are not getting referrals from female clients, assess your connection and strengthen trust.

2. **Get feedback.** Initiate service-oriented questions that confirm and strengthen your service bond.

3. **Develop referral process.** Devise interest-probing questions that open opportunities into her network and encourage viral marketing.

4. **Follow their lead.** Pursue marketing opportunities into women's networks as they are offered.

Personal Goals & Action Steps

Use the chart below to enter goals, action steps and target dates related to your goals

#1 Goal	→ #2 Action Steps	→ #3 Target Date

Bibliography

Barber, Brad M. and Terrance Odean. 2001. Boys will be boys: gender, overconfidence, and common stock investment. *The Quarterly Journal of Economics* February: 261-292.

Basham, Megan. 2008. Who wears the pants. *The Wall Street Journal*, October 10.

Bhonslay, Marianne. 2008. Power play: The women's market is scoring with innovation, branding and rising sales. *Sporting Goods Business*, 41 (3): 18.

Bowen, John J. 2006. Women of wealth. *Financial Planning*, November 2006.

Cavallari, Renie. 2008. Hint: It's more business than you might think. *Hotel & Motel Management* 223 (8): 16.

Cincotta, Katie. 2007. What women want from brands. *B&T Weekly*, August 24.

Denmark, Frances. 2008. Alpha Females. *Institutional Investor*, September.

Dorfman, Rich. 2007. Taking care of business. *Bank Marketing* 39 (8): 22-28.

Feiring, Alice. 2006. Of wine and women. *Time* 167 (15): B1.

Field, Katherine. 2008. Hardware's softer side. *Chain Store Age* 84 (3): 80-82.

Florian, Amy. 2008. Call me anytime-Effectively helping grieving clients will help you retain business. *Financial Advisor Magazine.* December.

Gladwell, Michael. 2005 *Blink: the power of thinking without thinking.* New York: Little, Brown & Co., Time Warner Book Group.

Gundeck, Caroline N. 2005. Women and wealth. Illinois CPA Society. http://www.icpas.org/hc-publications.aspx?id=5339&linkidentifier=id &itemid=5339 (accessed August 20, 2009).

Hall, John R. 2007. Contractor strategies of marketing to women. *Air Conditioning Heating & Refrigeration News,* 232 (9): 9.

Hamilton, Anita. 2007. The money queens. *Time South Pacific,* April 16.

Hersch, Warren S. 2008. Reaching boomer women – first through the heart. *National Underwriter,* November 17.

Kavovit, Barbara. 2006. Women aren't just smaller versions of men. *Aftermarket Business* 116 (1): 26.

Kruger, Jennifer B. 2005. Meeting a higher standard: women consumers spend more and demand more than men. Delight them, and they're yours forever. *Photo Marketing* 80 (11): 17.

LeBlanc, Sydney. 2006. The Mayo Clinic of wealth management. In "The wealth factor: a team approach, pub. *Financial Forum Inc.* 113-114.

Leder, Gerri. 2007. Teaching on the job. *On Wall Street,* October.

Lee, Jeanne. 2008. Women's work. *Financial Planning,* March.

Loibl, Cazilia and Tahira K. Hira. 2007. New insights into advising female clients on Investment Decisions. *Journal of Financial Planning,* March.

Bibliography

McBreen, Catherine S. and George H. Walper, Jr. 2007. Guiding the affluent women. *On Wall Street*, December.

Marketing to Women: Addressing women and women's sensibilities, January 2007. 20 (1): 2. Technology companies court women with advertising, special features and lots and lots of pink.

Marketing to Women: Addressing women and women's sensibilities, January 2007. 20 (1): 4. For female readers, sex bores.

Marketing to Women: Addressing women and women's sensibilities, January 2007. 20 (1): 5. Moms have their own generation gap.

Marketing to Women: Addressing women and women's sensibilities, February 2007. 20 (2): 5. For female shoppers, price matters.

Marketing to Women: Addressing women and women's sensibilities, May 2007. 20 (5): 6. All about women consumers.

Marketing to Women: Addressing women and women's sensibilities, June 2007. 20 (6):1. Women are clicking: the online world becomes a vital platform for reaching female consumers of all ages.

Marketing to Women: Addressing women and women's sensibilities, June 2007. 19 (19): 12. Nine in 10 women recommend products.

Marketing to Women: Addressing women and women's sensibilities, March 2006. 19 (3): 1. Women appreciate technology but aren't early adopters.

Marketing to Women: Addressing women and women's sensibilities, July 2006. 19 (7):1.Selling to women requires good listening skills and a strategy of helping, rather than pushing.

Marketing to Women: Addressing women and women's sensibilities, July 2006. 19 (7): 2. AXA tailors sales to women.

Marketing to Women: Addressing women and women's sensibilities, November 2006. 19 (11): 1. Word of mouth and cause marketing are key tools for bringing women (back) to destination spas.

Marketing to Women: Addressing women and women's sensibilities, March 2005. 18 (3): 1. Women's market gains recognition; women seek control over their time. Meagher, Lisa. 2006. What women want: how to recruit and keep women customers. *Community Banker,* April.

Meyers, Tiffany. 2006. She-noms: They're not your mother's consumer; wake up and straighten out the jargon of tech toys, select the beer of fashion week. *Advertising Age* 77 (44): S-1.

MIT Age Lab. 2008. Why women worry. http://web.mit.edu/agelab/projects_retirement shtl#whywomenworry (accessed January 2009).

New Media Age. In brief: women go online for trustworthy car advice. January 12, 2006.

O'Brien, Elizabeth. 2007. He said, she said. *Financial Planning,* June.

O'Brien, Elizabeth. 2006. Testing the glass ceiling-women are working to raise their numbers-and their profile-in the financial industry. *Financial Planning,* November.

Oppenheimer Funds. Women & investing. Survey 2007.

Palmer, Kimberly. 2008. How banks should talk to women. MSN Money and US News & World Report. http://articles.moneycentral.msn.com/savinganddebt/consumeractionguide (accessed July 10, 2008).

Powell, Robert. 2009. Keeping the glass filled – "Divide and conquer" couples best at retirement planning. MarketWatch. http://www.marketwatch.com/news/story/divide-conquer-couples-best- retirement/story (accessed February 25, 2008).

Roberts, Philippa. 2007. Forget the spare rib. Think profits. *Marketing Week*, February 8. Roberts, Sam. 2007. 51% of women are now living without spouse. NYTimes.com. http://www.nytimes.com/2007/01/16/us/16census.html (accessed October 22, 2008).

Rappaport, Anna. 2008. Addressing women's unique concerns. *Investment News,* July 17.

Seneca, Lucius Annaeus. The Quotations Page. http://www.quotationspage.com/quote 4576.html (accessed May 2009).

Stallard, Michael Lee, with Carolyn Dewing-Hommes and Jason Pankau. 2007. *Fired up or burned out: how to reignite your team's passion, creativity, and Productivity.* Nashville, TN: Thomas Nelson.

Stanny, Barbara. 2007. Seminar selling to women. *Advisor Today* 102 (5): 46-48.

Styring, Kelly. 2008. 50 plus, footloose & flush. *Brandweek* 49 (2): 7.

Swift, Marie. 2007. Beyond Mars and Venus. *Financial Planning* 37 (7): 64-69.

Tracey, Kevin and Carol Achterhof. 2007. Feminine Allure. *Bank Marketing* 39 (8): 18-21.

Ursiny, Timothy E., with Gary DeMoss and James Morel. 2006. *Coaching the sale: discovering the issues, discussing solutions and deciding on outcome!* Naperville, IL. Sourcebooks, Inc.

U.S. Census Bureau. 2006. Unmarried and single Americans week September 17-23. Percentage of unmarried and single Americans who are women. http://www.census.gov/pressrelease/www/releases/archives/families_households/ 006840.html (accessed October 22, 2008).

Vence, Deborah L. 2007. Untapped market. *Marketing News* 41 (14): 28.

What's a Trillion? http://frugaldad.com/2009/01/28/an-american-bailout-
1-million-a-day-for-2740-years/
http://help.lockergnome.com/office2/Autonumber-Drastic-Increase--
ftopict802561.html
http://thedametruth.net/wordpress/:
http://www.ehd.org/science_technology_largenumbers.php

Young, Diane. 2008. Building a female-friendly practice. *National Underwriter*,
November 3.

Zweig, Jason. 2009. For Mother's Day, giver her reins to the portfolio. The Wall Street Journel. http://onlinewsj.com/article_email/
SB124181915279001967 (accessed May 29, 2009).

About the Authors

Barbara A. Kay, MA, LPC, RCC

As President of Barbara Kay Coaching, Barbara serves clients through coaching, consulting and speaking on individual and relational core competencies including: time, teams, coaching, client relationships, attitude, change, behavioral finance, communication, motivation, productivity and leadership.

Barbara completed graduate and post-graduate training in Clinical Psychology and Coaching. She is a Registered Corporate Coach through the Worldwide Association of Business Coaches and is a Certified Trainer of the Registered Corporate Coach program. Her publications include numerous articles and the book, *The Top Performer's Guide to Change*. Barbara is a speaking guest for regional and national financial services organizations, industry partners and associations.

To learn more about coaching, consulting and presentations visit the website at www.barbarakaycoaching.com. For timely tips and tools visit Barbara's blog at www.barbarakay.wordpress.com

Tony DiLeonardi, RCC

With sales management experience dating back to 1987, Anthony J. DiLeonardi plays a key role in the determination of overall corporate strategies and business development and is responsible for the creation of business-development programs for Claymore Securities, an investment firm near Chicago, Illinois. He also works with the firm's strategic partners and financial advisors.

Tony is Vice Chairman at Claymore and is responsible for content and programs delivered by Claymore Securities to the financial professional to maximize their personal and professional productivity. Much of this content is geared toward helping financial advisors become more efficient in their ability to deliver superior service and investment management to their valued clients. Tony speaks regularly at Claymore productivity enhancement meetings throughout North America in which he shares his passion for helping financial advisors maximize their potential.

Tony previously served as Claymore's Senior Managing Director, Distribution, where he was responsible for packaged products distribution and national account relationships. He graduated from Illinois State University with a Bachelor's degree in Communications and is Series 7, 24 and 63 registered.

37037054R00093

Made in the USA
Charleston, SC
24 December 2014